THERE'S
NO PLAN B
FOR YOUR
A-GAME

I dedicate this book to my dad,
Charles Eason,
for what he saw in me that I
couldn't see for myself.

THERE'S NO PLAN B FOR YOUR A-GAME

Be the Best in the World at What You Do

BO EASON

St. Martin's Press
New York

THERE'S NO PLAN B FOR YOUR A-GAME. Copyright © 2019 by DB21, Inc.
All rights reserved. Printed in the United States of America. For information, address
St. Martin's Publishing Group, 120 Broadway, New York, NY 10271.

www.stmartins.com

The Library of Congress Cataloging-in-Publication Data is available upon request.

ISBN 978-1-250-21082-1 (hardcover)
ISBN 978-1-250-21084-5 (ebook)

Our books may be purchased in bulk for promotional, educational, or business use.
Please contact your local bookseller or the Macmillan Corporate and Premium Sales
Department at 1-800-221-7945, extension 5442, or by email at
MacmillanSpecialMarkets@macmillan.com.

First Edition: September 2019

10 9 8 7 6 5 4 3 2 1

CONTENTS

ACKNOWLEDGMENTS

No one wins alone.

When you begin your journey toward being the best, it is a lonely road. And then something strange begins to happen. A whole slew of smart people come out of nowhere to help you, guide you, mentor you, and clear the forest for you. The writing of this book was no exception.

I'd like to thank Celeste Fine and Sarah Passick at Park & Fine Literary and Media for believing in the book and J. J. Virgin for challenging me to write it.

I'm grateful for my publishing partnership with George Witte and his team at St. Martin's Press.

This book would never have come to fruition without the skill and determination of Karen Lacey and Kim Castleberry. Thank you.

To all my teammates and coaches from Delta High School to UC Davis, from the Houston Oilers to the

San Francisco 49ers, thank you for teaching me how to compete.

To my mentors and teachers, Jean-Louis Rodrigue, Larry Moss, Roy London, Breck Costin, and Brendon Burchard, thank you for helping me find my voice.

Thanks to my mom, my brother, and my sisters for always protecting my dreams and having the patience to allow me to find my way.

Finally to my wife, Dawn, who always says yes to my crazy dreams and then brings them into existence. I love you and I love building things with you, especially our kids. And to my kids, Eloise, Axel, and Lyla, thanks for allowing Daddy to use you as guinea pigs to test out my principles of what it takes to be the best. I can't wait to watch your lives unfold!

THERE'S
NO PLAN B
FOR YOUR
A-GAME

1.

THE BEGINNING OF THE BEST

The first time I ever played tackle football, the very first day of practice, they weighed and measured us for the game program. I was a freshman in high school, five feet tall, one hundred pounds, and by the look on the coach's face, it was clear I was not football material.

My dad picked me up after practice, and I told him, "Dad, they weighed and measured us, and the coach thinks I'm too small to play."

Without skipping a beat, he said, "Did they measure your heart, goddammit?"

I told him, "My school doesn't even have one of those heart-measuring things."

Then my dad told me a story about a little puppy. He was a ranch hand on his uncle's cattle ranch, and they used a dog to help them herd the cattle. This dog was amazing. It could do the work of ten men, and it was always one step ahead of the herd. The ranch literally could not survive without this dog. "When the ranch dog gets too old and loses a step, they breed it with another rancher's dog," my dad said. "And then when the puppies are born, the rancher takes the smallest puppy, the runt of the litter, and ties a little piece of yarn around its neck. Then he watches that puppy very carefully. After about twelve weeks, the rancher takes all the puppies except for the runt and gives them away. The runt of the litter is the new working dog on the ranch.

"Bo, the runt always has to work harder to survive against its bigger brothers and sisters. Always. The runt becomes the smartest, the fastest, the most determined. Of all the puppies, the runt's heart is the biggest. The rancher stakes his whole livelihood on that fact.

"Bet on the runt every time, goddammit."

I knew what my dad was telling me. I'm the youngest of six kids, so I knew my place. I was the runt. I had to work harder than anyone else. And that's exactly what I did. I made that dog's story my story. And I've been telling myself that story ever since. It helped me develop the stamina to keep going after what I wanted most in life, and it led to every success I've ever had.

Story. Stamina. Success. It's that simple.

That doesn't mean it's easy. It can be hard as hell to keep repeating your story and to follow through with the actions that will make the story come true. But I know you can do it. Because if I did it, anyone can do it.

Now, I don't pretend I know your story. But I do know this:

You will succeed or fail based on the stories you tell yourself and others.

My dad was a cowboy—a real-life, working cowboy. You've probably got a picture already of what sort of person that would be: gruff, no-nonsense, practical. Finished every sentence with a cussword as if it were punctuation.

Yet every morning, my dad woke my brother, Tony, and me saying, "Keep moving, partner. You're the best in there, goddammit. You're the best."

You're the best. He massaged that message into our brains everywhere we went, from the Little League baseball field, to getting on the school bus, to the time we went on a double date with the Tomasini sisters in high school. Every morning, every evening, for twenty years, he continued. He saw greatness in us that we just couldn't see for ourselves. My brother and I were embarrassed that he would say it right in front of our friends and teammates and dates. And then one day, years later, we thought, *Well, maybe he's right. Maybe we are the best.* My brother and I surrendered to what he saw in us, and we lived into our own greatness. He spoke us into existence.

Ever since my childhood, I've been obsessed with what makes people great, what makes them the best. And because of that obsession, I inherited my dad's best quality: the ability to see greatness in people and speak it into existence. I can show anyone who has the guts to commit—anyone who will choose the pain of discipline over the pain of regret—how to become a top performer. It takes commitment, and it takes focus, and it takes the willingness to drop anything that does not serve your mission.

If you fully commit yourself, you can be the best in the world at what you do. Don't believe me? Well, think about this: You were born the best. Do you remember the day of your conception? If you don't, let me remind you of what happened on that day. On the day you were conceived, three hundred million sperm were released. The sperm that would help create you was one of those. Three hundred million sperm backed by millions of years of evolution, designed to accomplish one thing—penetrate an egg. All three hundred million have one job. And one of those sperm got the job done.

So you tell me, who won the first race you ever entered? *You.* You, I—we won that race with three-hundred-million-to-one odds against us. We come into this world with greatness already sewn into the fabric of our DNA. We just need to acknowledge our potential and remember and surrender to who we already are.

I'm proof that this attitude can succeed.

At the age of nine, I declared I wanted to play pro football. I took a crayon and a piece of school paper, and I drew up a twenty-year plan. And this plan wasn't just about getting into the NFL. This plan was going to make me into the best safety in the world.

That plan ruled my life. For the next nine years, I woke up every morning at 5:00 to run drills (which in this case meant running backward, because safeties do a lot of that). *Everything* I did was with that NFL dream in mind. If an activity or an event didn't move me along my path to being the best safety in the world, I didn't do it. Prom? Nope. Goofing around? Nope. I was focused, and I was dead serious. This was my life dream, after all—crayon and everything.

So by the end of my senior year in high school, you'd think at least one college would recruit me, one school would offer me a football scholarship, right?

Wrong.

Not a single college in the entire country was interested. Three hundred fifty colleges and universities in this nation play football, and not one of them wanted me.

So I invited myself to a small college near my hometown. I had my plan, right? And after nine years of running backward as fast as I could, I wasn't going to suddenly stop because no one wanted me.

I enrolled at the University of California–Davis, which gave zero scholarships and played Division II football. I just showed up at their training camp a month before classes started. I talked my way into a uniform, a meal ticket, and dorm keys from the equipment managers. Kept my dream alive, right? It was all going according to my plan.

Maybe not. I was sent home after the first day of practice. They took back my uniform, my meal ticket, and

my dorm keys. I spent the night in my truck, eating peanut butter–hot dog bun sandwiches.

The next day, I showed up in the locker room as if
nothing had happened and begged the equipment managers to give me another uniform—just give me a chance
to prove myself—and for whatever reason, they agreed.
They gave me an ancient hunk of cloth that might have
been a uniform at one time. They handed over the biggest helmet I'd ever seen. Every step I took, it bounced
down over my eyes. I put on that non-matching uniform
and that helmet, and I showed up for practice every day,
twice a day. And then I slept in my truck and ate peanut
butter–hot dog bun sandwiches.

I did that for a solid month, and eventually, I played
my way onto that team because I refused to quit. I refused
to believe that nine years of getting up at 5:00 every morning and running backward as fast as I could hadn't been
worth it. I had faith in myself and my plan, even when
no one else did.

Four years later, the Houston Oilers drafted me as a
top safety taken during the 1984 NFL draft. After four
years with Houston, I was traded to the San Francisco
49ers. Then a career-ending knee injury knocked me
out of football—and onto the operating table for the
seventh time—and out of the only life I'd ever known or
planned for.

I knew instantly that I was in deep trouble. I had no
Plan B. I'd never planned for anything other than playing pro football, and I had no option other than playing

pro football. What was I? I was the best in the world at running my head into other people at twenty-five miles an hour. That ability does not translate to civilian life.

So there I was. My knee and my career were smashed beyond repair. I knew I'd be wheeled off the field and into surgery. And I realized, lying there in that pileup on an NFL field, that all the energy and drive I'd channeled into football needed to be redirected, or I'd end up in prison. I needed a new twenty-year plan, one that used my body's energy, my innate command to *move* and make impact.

And right there, as I was being wheeled off the field, I decided I'd go to New York City and work with acting coaches who could teach me how to use my body to communicate from a stage. I have no idea where this idea came from, but I went with it. I decided to learn how to speak to people, to express myself both physically and with words.

So I moved to New York and found the best acting and movement coaches available. I took every class I could find. And I decided I needed a new life plan (one not written with crayon this time). And that plan was to be the best stage performer of our time.

So I asked all the people in classes with me, "Who's the greatest stage performer of all time?" and they all said, "Al Pacino." Obviously, I needed to meet Al Pacino. I just needed to figure out how to make that happen.

A couple of days later, I was having dinner with a friend. Anna Strasberg, Lee Strasberg's widow, was in the restaurant. My friend knew Anna and introduced me to her. So I did what I do, which is ask questions. Here's the widow of the best acting coach in the world—of course I was going to learn whatever I could. How could I be the best? What should I do? What would Lee have told me to do?

Turned out Anna liked me because I asked all these questions about how to improve my acting. It also turned out that Al Pacino is the godfather for her two sons. When I heard that, I immediately asked for an introduction to him. I told Anna that I wanted what Al Pacino had. I wanted to be the best stage actor, so I needed to find out what he did.

Anna agreed to introduce us, which is how I ended up playing touch football in the snow with her two sons and Al Pacino and then went to his house, where he spent three hours breaking down the next fifteen years for me.

I told Al, "All the kids in my acting classes tell me you're the best stage actor of our time. I want that. Can you tell me how to do that?"

And he said, "Yeah, I can tell you. But you might not like the answer, because it's going to take you fifteen years."

I said, "Cool. I work really well with that sort of time-line." Obviously, Al didn't know about my crayon-and-paper twenty-year plan. Fifteen years would be a snap.

Al Pacino told me I had to get onstage—any stage, anywhere, as often as I could. We spent three hours playing pool and laying out a road map for my success. And at the end, I thanked him, and I said, "You must get this sort of question all the time from actors."

"No, you're the first," he said. "I have actors ask me how to get famous, or can I get them a part, or can I introduce them to my agent. You're the only one who's ever asked how to be the best."

The fifteen-year plan Al dictated to me was pretty simple. Basically, I had to spend more time on a stage than anyone else in the world. So I did. I spent the next fifteen years acting anywhere I could get a role, starting with a children's play in Sacramento, California.

That's right. From competing against and playing with the top athletes in the world, I went to acting in a kids' play, *The Shoemaker and the Elves*. I was the mayor of the town, and I wore this big silly hat, and I was acting with a bunch of kids. I'd gone from signing autographs in NFL stadiums to standing in front of a hundred noisy kids who were not even looking at me. They were too busy shoving each other and eating popcorn.

At one point during the play, I looked out into the audience and saw my brother, Tony, and my friend and ex-roommate, Kenny O'Brien, sitting there. They showed up to support me, which was great. So you have to picture this: These guys are both NFL quarterbacks. Tony had just taken the New England Patriots to the Super Bowl, and Kenny was the starting quarterback of the New York Jets. They're huge guys sitting in these kid-sized seats, and they're looking at me like they're just totally in shock. Like they were thinking, *Good job with the mayor's hat, Bo, but what the hell are you doing and why?*

But I knew what I was doing. I had my fifteen-year plan. This kids' play was just part of the process.

I knew that my mastery as an NFL safety didn't mean I could walk into any acting job anywhere and be great. My football skills did not transfer to acting. But my ability to focus, practice, rehearse, and keep my plan in mind at all times *did* transfer. I just needed another long-term plan with a different goal, one that focused on acting, movement, and writing plays.

So I did what Al Pacino told me to do. I got on every stage I could. I rehearsed constantly. Everything I did related to my new long-term plan. Eventually, I wrote and staged a one-person semiautobiographical play called *Runt of the Litter* (it's now being adapted as a major motion picture). In 2004, *The New York Times* referred to it as "one of the most powerful plays in the last decade." But you know the best review I ever received? One night, about ten or fifteen minutes into the play, I made eye contact with a man sitting on the aisle, about five rows back. He crossed his arms over his chest and gave me an approving nod.

That guy was Al Pacino.

I performed *Runt* for fifteen years, 1,300 performances. By this time, I was married, and my wife, Dawn, and I took the show on a fifty-city tour across the country. And after a while, something odd started to happen. Businesspeople started knocking on my stage door. They always asked the same thing: "Can you bring this to my company? I want my employees to see your play."

I always had the same answer: "What the hell? No. This is a theater piece."

They kept asking, and I kept saying no. Finally, one executive offered to fly me, Dawn, and the kids (we had two at this point) to Hawaii if I would perform *Runt* at his company's one-hundred-year anniversary celebration. He named an enormous speaker fee. After I picked my jaw up off the floor, I finally understood what was going on. These business executives didn't want their employees to have a theater experience; *they wanted their employees to adopt my mind-set.*

That's when a huge light went on for me. I saw that I could reach thousands more people—*tens of thousands* more people—as a speaker and trainer than as an actor. I could have impact on a scale I'd never dreamed of. I could help people actually change their lives if I shifted my goal from acting to outreach.

I needed a new plan.

This third time around, I knew exactly how to become the best speaker and trainer in the world: I needed to tell myself a different story.

That was the moment when I realized everything I'd accomplished was because of the stories I was telling myself. I just had to follow the same process I'd used in my NFL career and my theater career. This wasn't about natural talent; it was about eliminating everything that didn't support my new story and focusing every day on making that new story happen.

If I didn't realize it before, I got it now. It doesn't matter what you want to do. Let me repeat that. *It doesn't matter what you want to do.* It only matters what story you tell yourself and then how you live out that story, every single day, until you gain mastery. And every day after that, as well.

Sound intimidating? Well, I'm not going to sugarcoat the truth. And if you've read this far, you know I'm not offering you a quick-fix, thirty-day-miracle life turnaround.

It's not easy. It's not always fun. It might involve peanut butter–hot dog bun sandwiches; it definitely will involve focus and effort and stamina. And it can be scary as hell—trusting your gut, refusing to stay with the pack. But the results I've seen, and the results my clients have seen, prove that it's worthwhile.

Before I outline, step by step, how you're going to change your life, let's go back to the very beginning for this one.

When I was in high school, there were 1.2 million high school football players in the United States. What percentage of those 1.2 million players do you suppose went on to play in the NFL? Answer: 0.03 percent.

My tiny high school had twenty-seven boys—farm boys—on the football team. There had never been a pro athlete from that high school before I got there, and never one since I left. Not one. Based on the statistics I just showed you of high school players turning pro, how many of those twenty-seven farm boys on my team do you suppose went on to play in the NFL?

Answer: Four. Four of us played in the NFL for a total of twenty-five years, with two Super Bowl appearances. That's a statistical impossibility. That can't happen. Especially given that there's never been a history at the school for pro athletes of any kind. So how do you explain it? Coincidence? Something in the water? Sheer dumb luck?

I'm convinced it's none of those things. It's the power of having someone around who was so focused on his dream and his plan that maybe he inspired other boys to go along with him.

A while back, I was at a class reunion, and I asked a couple of the other guys why they thought we all went on to play in the pros. And they told me, "Hey, you were running around with your twenty-year plan, and we figured if that little shit Bo was gonna play in the NFL, we could, too."

After that class reunion, I was thinking about the roommates I've had and how I might have influenced them without knowing it. My first-ever roommate, my brother, Tony, was a first-round quarterback pick in the NFL draft. He led the New England Patriots to their first Super Bowl. My first college roommate, Kenny O'Brien, was also a first-round quarterback pick. Two roommates, two first-round draft picks as quarterbacks. Don't you know everyone was lining up to be my roommate now!

My second college roommate was a sixth-round quarterback pick. I'm three for three with roommates becoming NFL quarterbacks! And Dawn, my fourth and final roommate, became a Hollywood and Broadway producer. I'm not saying I caused their success. They were the ones who put in the work. They were the ones who focused and ran the miles. But you've got to admit there are some very strange coincidences going on here that defy all statistical possibilities. Did I have influence on them? Could my own focus and commitment have helped sharpen theirs?

Just think of the impact you can have on the important people in your life.

I'm only going to make you one promise: If you do what I say, or more important, if you do what I do, people will not have the ability to look away from you. You will lead in ways you never expected, and it will transform you. It will transform your entire life and all your relationships. You will have such deep impact on the people closest to you that they'll tell their own stories and find their way to the top right along with you.

But it will only happen if you commit to giving everything you've got for as long as it takes to work through this book. I'm going to help you find your story, build the stamina it takes to live it, and guide you to success. Just like my dad started every day for me by telling me I was the best, I'm here to tell you you're the best. I'm telling you it's time for you to tell a new story about yourself.

Let's get started.

ACTION STEP

Write who you are and where you see your life heading. Keep this short—no more than about a page. This book is about transforming yourself, so you need to know where you're starting. By the way, that piece of paper with my twenty-year plan written in crayon? I still have it, and you will want to keep yours.

For more questions to ask yourself about who you are and where you're headed in the future, check out boeason.com/actionsteps.

2.

UNNATURAL TALENT

By now, you probably understand why I don't believe in natural talent, even though you've heard it all your life, when people talk about musicians or athletes or artists. "Oh, she's a natural." "He's so gifted." "Sure wish I could run like that! You have to be *born* that fast."

I'm here to tell you that's the wrong story to tell about super-high achievers, for a couple of reasons. First, the only "natural" thing about talented people is that they're using their natural human ability to adapt. They place themselves beyond their current capacity, and they practice outside of their comfort zone until their body adapts. That's how they get better and better and eventually reach the top. They practice, and then they practice some more. Anyone can do that (even though most people don't—but we'll come back to that later in the book). Science has proven that there are "no shortcuts and no prodigies," as Anders Ericsson would say.

Second, when you dismiss someone's success as being due to some magical "natural talent" that they were born with and you weren't, you have just cut your own throat. You've just eliminated yourself from the game. Stop it. Stop it! Time for you to take your life into your own hands. Being the best is your responsibility, your birthright. One day you're going to be standing on the very top and people will try to ignore the hours and years and sweat and concentration you've put in because they don't want to pay the price of greatness themselves. They're telling themselves the wrong story.

You know how people burst into prominence in sports or the arts and everyone says, "Oh, they're so gifted"? No. What you're actually seeing is someone who has been deliberately busting their ass for a decade or two. What's invisible to everyone is all those dark, early mornings, cold, alone, hands on knees, bent over from exhaustion. That's our story.

I've seen that play out in my own family. Growing up on a ranch, we didn't have a television that got much reception, any cell phones, and certainly had no video games. So for hours every day, my brother would throw me the football, and I would catch it. We had fun; it was hard work but immensely rewarding, and it paid off. We were both top draft picks into the NFL. But you know what they said about my brother when he was selected in the first round of the NFL draft as a quarterback? "Oh, he's so naturally gifted. I mean, he just picked up a ball and could throw." And about me, they said, "Oh, he's naturally fast. He has an innate talent for tracking down the ball." Those sorts of remarks take away from the hours we put in. There's no gene for working to bring something rewarding into existence. There's no inherited talent for discipline. I don't get to say, "I'm disciplined and you're not." That's not true. What is true is that I trained myself to put in the hours it takes to master a skill, whether it was football or playwriting or performing or public speaking. That's not a talent. It's a skill, and it can be learned.

I'm prepared for the same thing to happen with my son, Axel. At the age of six, Axel wrote down his plan. He wants to play in both the NBA and the NFL. No one has ever accomplished that feat. Here are the odds of that happening: If Axel plays football in high school (he's only twelve now), he'll have a 0.03 percent chance of playing in the NFL. If he plays high school basketball, he'll have a 0.03 percent chance of playing in the NBA. The chances of him playing in both the NFL and the NBA are 0.00 percent. No one's ever done it. There is no data; there is no percentage. I know this may sound crazy to you, but I think he's going to do it. When people hear of his dream, they say it's impossible and they can't see how it can be accomplished. To me, it's as clear and as predictable as the nose on my face, because he has all the principles in place to be the best. And in ten years' time, when he does accomplish that dream, you know what they'll say about him?

"Oh, he's naturally gifted. His dad played in the NFL. His uncle played in the NFL. What a lucky kid to get those genes." The fact is that this kid, for half his life at this point, has been focused on and working toward something that's never been done. He hasn't won some genetic lottery. He's not lucky or gifted. What he is, is focused and committed and loyal to something. He told himself a story he believes in, and every day he puts in the work to fulfill that story.

I assume you're reading this book because the story "I'm not naturally talented so I can't be the best" or "There's nothing I can do to change" or "I'm not good enough" no longer works for you. You have to know what story is running your life before you can tell yourself a different story and change your life.

Here's what I mean: So many of us are just unconsciously living out the story that we've adopted from someone else. So if the family story is "Hey, we have a lot of alcoholics in our family" or "Oh, we don't make much money in this family," then if you don't examine that story, you go along and live with that story. We use the story as a survival mechanism.

So if we're the authors of our own stories, why would we write a lousy story? Why don't we write a great one? Why don't we write a thriller or a romantic love story or an Olympic gold champion story? Why do we so often write a story about "Oh, I'm not that good," "Oh, I can't do that," and other stories that don't demand the best of us? It can be scary demanding the best from ourselves

100 percent of the time, and that's why most people don't do it. But I'm here to show you how to do it.

This is the chapter where we start to work on your mind shift. You are going to begin to see what I see. You are going to change the way you think. You are going to change the story you tell yourself. And then you're going to start living out that story in your life, step by step.

You can be a leader and be the best at what you do. This belief drives everything in my life. Just like I don't believe anyone is naturally gifted, I also believe that there are no natural leaders. My mission is to bring out greatness in people who have the stamina and courage to fulfill their destiny and achieve their highest possible success. I challenge those people to become leaders and embrace their "unnatural talent."

We are talking about greatness here. And there's nothing more attractive than greatness. People say to me, "I want to be in a committed relationship, Bo." And I say, "Oh, really? So how are your commitments looking? Are you fully committed to a thing? Because if you want people to be attracted to you, or money to be attracted to you, or opportunities to be attracted to you, you'd better get your ass committed. You'd better attempt to be the best in the world at a thing. Then watch what happens. Because people are drawn to that effort, that courage. It is always rewarded in this lifetime."

For many of us, this book will be the first time anyone has said to you, "You are the best." It will be the first time anyone has had that faith in you and demanded that you rise above your fear.

It's the first time anyone has told you, "Don't be okay with being comfortable. You can do better than that. Yeah, you have to step outside your comfort zone (I warned you this book was not going to be easy, remember?). You have to change how you're approaching your life, starting with identifying and then changing the story you tell."

But I know you can do it. And science proves it. We know that the animals who survive long term are not the smartest or the biggest. The ones who survive long term are the ones who can adapt the fastest.

And if you can understand and then change your story, you can adapt.

It's not just me telling you this. It's experts such as K. Anders Ericsson, who's been studying human performance since the 1980s. His most recent book, *Peak: Secrets from the New Science of Expertise,* explains the process of deliberate practice. Deliberate practice is a combination of repeated action and strong mental representations—in other words, action plus story equals expertise. This method has been shown to be more successful than the simple "ten-thousand-hour rule" that's been popularized. When you tell yourself your story and back it up with hours and months and years and decades of hard work, that's when you attain mastery.

Before we go any further, let me define what I mean by *hard work.* I'm probably using the term differently from how you are. I'm not talking about digging ditches or painting your house. I'm talking about focused, quality, rewarding effort and time that you put into moving yourself closer to your dream. So when you read *hard work* in this book, remember that's what I'm talking about.

Lauren Cheney Holiday

Lauren Cheney Holiday, known as "Chain" to her soccer teammates, is one of the most talented, hardworking, and respected athletes in the United States. I'm so grateful to tell part of her story in this book. She's the first women's soccer professional to have her jersey number retired, which tells you something about her impact on the game. A fierce competitor since she was a young child, Lauren had more than the normal number of hurdles to overcome before meeting her goal of playing in the Olympics and the World Cup. She continued facing major life challenges after retirement, as well.

I haven't worked with Lauren, but we take the same basic approach to becoming the best. Every single one of the steps I outline she did naturally, instinctively, and on her own. You can see from her experience that these tools can work for anyone. They'll work for you, whatever your goal is. I'll let Lauren tell part of her story here, and we'll hear more from her throughout the book.

Here's Lauren's story, told in her own words:

I was born with a hole in my heart and a vein in the wrong place. It went undiagnosed until a new pediatrician noticed my irregular heartbeat. The doctors monitored me and decided that surgery could be put off until I was a little older. When I was three years old, I had open heart surgery that fixed the hole in my heart and rerouted my pulmonary vein.

I was already potty trained by the time I had the surgery, and when I woke up, I had tubes in my nose and I was heavily medicated, and they had put a diaper on me. My mom said she knew I would be okay because the first thing I said was, "I want my panties."

The doctors told my mom to make sure I was active, because anything that made my heart stronger would be good for it. I played any sport, but mostly I wanted to play anything my brother played, and he ended up playing soccer. I was supercompetitive and played on boys' teams as well as girls' teams until I was about twelve years old. Then I tried out for another boys' team that was a little more elite than the one I'd been playing with, and I didn't make it. My parents knew, but didn't tell me, that it was because some of the other parents complained that they didn't want a girl on the team. When I found that out, many years later, I was like, "Why would you not tell me that?" My parents explained that they never wanted me to have an excuse. They wanted me to become a better player; they wanted me to keep trying and fighting for what I wanted.

For as long as I can remember, probably since I was five years old, I wanted to win an Olympic gold medal. When I first learned how to write cursive, I would sign my name and tell my mom, "This is going to be famous. I'm going to play in the Olympics." I made playbooks and drew out plays, and I had the Olympic rings on my playbooks. Soccer was my passion, and the Olympics were for the best of the best. I wanted to be the best. That was my standard.

I remember my mom telling me over and over from a very young age, like maybe three or four years old, "Lauren, you have to be humble." I asked her about that just a few years ago, and she told me it was because she knew I had the ability to not be humble because I was so competitive, and I was so invested in winning. I wanted to be the very best at everything, and she felt that I needed that reminder every day. I'm so grateful that my mom recognized that in me at such a young age that she was able to guide me away from it.

My dad was a construction worker, and during the winter in Indiana, there's not a lot of work in his industry. Sometimes it would be just my mom working, or when I was younger and I was sick, my mom didn't work so she could be at home with me, and my dad found work. Sometimes they were literally just trying to make sure we had food on the table. And they kept those struggles from us; they never told us about them. Recently, I learned that at one point they only had forty-five dollars in the bank.

I was so focused on my sports, I just didn't notice anything else. In junior high, I tried out for the Olympic Development Program team. If you make your state team, you can try out for the regional team, and then they pick girls from each region to make up the national team. I tried out every year, and I never made it.

I remember the first time I tried out and didn't make it, I just lay in bed crying and listening to Gloria Estefan's song "Reach." That sounds so cheesy, but it's about reaching higher. I was playing it on repeat, and I'm sure my parents thought I was crazy. I remember every time I tried out thinking, *I'm going to make it, I'm going to make it,* and I just never did. Then my freshman year in high school, the coach of the regional team asked me to go to California for an event. I ended up being our leading scorer, and I was the youngest player there. Greg Ryan was the under-twenty-one (U-21) national team coach, and he pulled me aside and said, "I want you on the team." So I never made the youth national team; I went straight onto the U-21 national team, which is right below the Olympic team. Within a year of my getting onto the U-21 team, Greg got the women's national team coaching position, and he called me to come to my first Olympic team camp.

I was terrified and just trying to figure out, *Okay, what happens now? I've gotten called into the national team, I'm seventeen years old, I'm going in with players that I've watched on television.* I was so nervous at that first camp that I would go to practice, I would eat, and then I would go back to my room and sleep. I tried to stay by myself. I was by far the youngest player there, so I tried to keep myself unknown. I remember thinking, *Don't speak unless spoken to; just listen to what they have to say. If they ask you a question, answer, but just pay attention.* A lot of these girls were either in their senior year of college or just out of college and in a professional league. I was trying to learn how to get along in that environment, because it was so different from a high school team or any team that I was the best player on. I went from being the top of my team to being the bottom, and that was humbling. One time, it was ninety-five degrees out, and I passed out because I was so dehydrated. When I came to, everything was normal, and the other players were joking around with me. But I thought, *They're never going to call me back. This is so embarrassing. How could I do this?* I did get called back in but didn't make an actual team roster for about another six months. So I was consumed with the idea that I had to continue to get better.

You can go into an environment like that and either just crumble or get a little bit better every time you play. Things that worked in high school didn't work anymore; the girls were smarter, they were faster, they were stronger. Being with them accelerated my game. It prepared me for the college game physically, but even more so, mentally. I got to see how women competed in comparison to how girls compete. And I got to absorb knowledge from so many athletes who were ahead of me physically and mentally in the game.

Eventually, I played on two World Cup teams and two Olympic teams, winning two Olympic gold medals and a World Cup title. In 2013, I married Jrue Holiday, an NBA player I had met while we were both UCLA students. I retired in October of 2015, after we won the

World Cup and after my professional season was over. It was extremely emotional for me, which surprised me, since I was at peace with my decision to retire; I'd accomplished my goals of winning both Olympic gold and a World Cup title and starting in both tournaments. It was the right time to leave and start a family, and at the end of January 2016, I got pregnant.

Everything was going according to plan. Or so I thought.

At first, I felt great. I had no morning sickness, I was training with Jrue, I was dabbling with the idea of running a marathon. But at around four or five months, weird things started to happen. I had trouble swallowing food: I had to tell myself to swallow. I had numbness on the right side of my face. When I worked out, my balance was completely off, which everyone said was just because I was pregnant and carrying all this front weight I'd never carried before. But after being an athlete for so many years, I was totally in tune with my body, and I knew something was wrong.

I went to three neurologists and got a diagnosis of probable MS from all of them, which surfaces in some women when they're pregnant. There's nothing you can do about it when you're pregnant; I'd have to wait to take MS medicine until after pregnancy. I wasn't satisfied with that diagnosis, but I figured after the baby was born, I could explore what was really happening. And then one night, I woke up with a horrific migraine, which is extremely unlike me. I don't even get headaches. I was at home alone in Louisiana, and Jrue was in California. At 3:00 in the morning, I decided I would demand an MRI.

My doctor agreed, and I went in for the MRI, even though I was pregnant. After taking the images, the MRI tech said to me, "Hang out here for a second, okay?"

I knew immediately that something was not right. The doctor called and said, "I have good news and bad news. The good news is you do not have MS. The bad news is you have a large brain tumor." I remember thinking that I couldn't even grasp what that meant.

My friend who had driven me to the hospital called Jrue right away and said, "Get your ass here now." He came home as soon as he could get a flight to New Orleans. I carried J.T. until I was thirty-five weeks pregnant, delivered her under general anesthesia, and had brain surgery four weeks later.

I think those months of pregnancy were the lowest I've ever been. My answer to every obstacle I've ever faced was to work harder or do something more. In this case, I couldn't do more. I needed to do less. I needed to rest, to relax, to give up control. That was hard enough, but the absolute hardest part was knowing that I had another human being inside of me. I remember thinking, *Whatever I have to do to keep her alive, to keep her safe, is what I do.* At around thirty-two weeks into the pregnancy, my migraines had worsened to the point of being unbearable. The tumor was continually growing because of my pregnancy hormones, but the pain of my migraines was so bad I told the doctor I didn't know how much longer I could do it. Then my neurosurgeon came in and told me that the difference in IQ between a thirty-two weeker and a thirty-five weeker was astronomical. He said, "If you can carry this baby for thirty-five weeks, you're giving her the best chance. We'll be here if you get worse."

From then on, I kept telling myself, *I'm going to make it to thirty-five weeks. It doesn't matter if I can't walk in a straight line, or if I'm falling over, or if my face is drooping. Whatever happens to me doesn't matter.* I moved to North Carolina about a month before I delivered just to ease my fear a bit, knowing I would be close to my neurologist and ob-gyn.

I had a C-section at thirty-five weeks. Somehow, I had convinced myself that if I made it to thirty-five weeks, my daughter would not have to go into the neonatal intensive care unit (NICU), and I assumed I'd take her home right after her birth. But J.T. got some fluid in her lungs, which often happens with C-section babies, and this on top of her being five weeks early, so she went straight into the NICU. In my mind, despite the fact J.T. was born a vibrant, healthy baby, I felt like I had failed. I felt extreme guilt. That week she spent in the NICU was the hardest week of my life. I felt like if I'd just made it to forty weeks, she would have been okay.

When I told my neurosurgeon this, he said, "I pushed you to the absolute last bit that you could have handled. You couldn't have carried her to forty weeks." That helped me feel better.

And after all of that, she is so great. She's smart and active and healthy, and everything is fine.

I'm not exactly sure what's next for me. My passion is people. I'm trying to figure out my next step. Where exactly can I have the most impact? I don't like recognition. I don't like the spotlight. I'd much rather be behind the scenes. I want to help people. I want to make the world better than it is, but I'm not 100 percent sure what that will look like. When I retired, I thought, *Oh, yeah, I'll have time to explore and really feel it out.* And then I got pregnant, and then I was diagnosed with a brain tumor. I feel like just now I'm ready to start exploring that again.

ACTION STEP

What do you want to accomplish? Write it down, and mentally put yourself there. Really feel yourself inhabiting your version of being the best.

Now, work your way backward from the point of your success. Write the story of the months and years of hard work you put in. The tears you cried in frustration when things went sideways. The struggles you had to keep going through. Your worst fears about everything bad that could happen. The hours you sweated and the times you quit. Write it all down. Now read it. You know what you've just written? You've written a story that has bumps and train wrecks and struggles all along the way, and yet you still triumph in the end. You're the best.

That's a story worth telling.

3.

DECLARATION

've always thought of the Declaration of Independence as a story. Nearly 250 years ago, the Founding Fathers declared who we were going to be as a country. Isn't that striking? Think about it. They declared it, and you and I and everyone around us are still living out that declaration every single day.

This is who we are, this is how we live, these are our values, this is what we believe, this is the freedom we claim—that story is brought to life on a daily basis because we continue to live out the Declaration of Independence.

I want you to think about your declaration as being similar to the Declaration of Independence. You're going to declare what you want to be the best at and live out of that declaration. Now, this is a very creative process. It's not like you have to state it a certain way, and you have to do this or write that. You do have to stay creative when you're making your declarations. Figure out what you want to be the best at. That's the hardest part; people usually want to choose several different things. So decide, and then get started on your artwork. You can see two declarations I made here—one from when I was nine years old, and that's pretty rudimentary artwork. It's forty-nine years old and falling apart. But this is what drove me. This was my idea of the best safety in the world.

The other one was my declaration for getting the play produced. The artwork on that one is a little better, but not fancy by any means.

So the declaration isn't a goal. Goals don't turn me on. That word is not powerful enough. I need to declare something, then live out of that declaration for the twenty years it will take to fulfill it. I've always done this through pictures, and that seems to work best for me. So I want you to draw, even if you think you're a horrible artist. Because there's power in the pictures that we draw of ourselves.

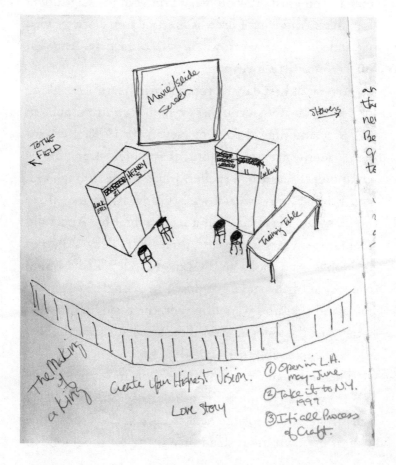

In 1998, Dawn and I were going to get married, and I announced to her that I was going to become a playwright. And she was like, "What?" And her family must have thought, *You're marrying who, and he's going to do what?*

I had never written anything. On my very first day of writing, I was sitting in a Barnes & Noble bookstore with a blank notebook and three hours on my parking meter. And I just drew out what I thought the stage might look like. And what I drew is pretty damn close to what we ended up with when we produced the play. And that play ran for fifteen years.

So on that first day, I wrote a bunch of stuff: "Making of a king, create your highest vision, love story, open in LA May and June. Take it to New York 1999." Remember, I'd never written anything in my life. I didn't have a computer. I was a bad speller. I just wrote it longhand, and I didn't know what I was writing. Every day, three hours a day, I created what a scene might be. And I did that for two years. Two years, three hours a day, at Barnes & Noble. And look, by the time March rolled around, the vision of the stage got down to a single locker and table and the titles were different, the dialogue was different, but the vision remained the same: to create the best piece of expression that I could.

Then it became pictures. There's us in Little League. There's my dad behind a chain-link fence. So, this told me what I was doing for the next twenty years. I took control of my own life instead of waiting for the phone to ring, instead of waiting for somebody to choose me. That's sports, really, and that's acting. "Somebody just choose me, and I'll get to be on your team. I'll get to be on your show." But if you choose yourself and you declare what you're going to be the best at, you should start living this life of going toward things instead of waiting. Now your future is coming at you just as fast as you're going at it. So you start to dress like the best safety in the world, and you start to say the things the best safety in the world says, and you start to act like the best safety in the world, and you train like the best safety in the world. You see what I mean? You're living this life instead of having a checklist of what you have to do today. You already know what the best safety in the world has to do today. You start to live that life, and yes, it takes years, obviously. But things start to happen, and your life is propelled forward.

I wrote this play declaration in 1998. I've never waited for the phone to ring since then. I just took my life in my own hands and said, "This is who I am, and this is where I want to be." From that day forward, everyone had to come to me. You know why? Because I created something. I used to be jealous of Tom Cruise and Nicolas Cage and Brad Pitt and James Franco for taking the roles that I wanted. I was trained enough, I was good enough to play, and they took those roles, and I said, "Forget them. I'm going to create something, and they are going to come to me." And, sure enough, who is my audience when I'm performing my play? Brad Pitt, Tom Cruise,

Nicolas Cage, and James Franco in the front row. Leonardo DiCaprio, Tobey Maguire. They're all in the fricking front row, and guess what they want? Me. Because I took my life in my own hands. They can't write, or they don't think they can write, and they don't think they can create. They have to wait for a writer to show up and choose them.

So, you make your declaration and own it. Now you live out that life, and all the things that support that life have to come to you because you're the one who created it. Hundreds of people were employed because of *Runt of the Litter.* One day it was just Dawn and me showing up, doing this play. The next day, we were in New York and there must have been a hundred people on the set being employed by me because I wrote something. You see what I mean?

It's crazy to think about, the power that a really big declaration has. Let's go back to my high school: Four guys from my high school football team played in the pros. There'd never been a pro player before I went there. There's never been one since I left. But four guys got supermotivated because of one kid who had a declaration, a dream. That's it. So, people come with you, and you employ a whole bunch of people who wouldn't have had that life had you not declared what you want to be the best at.

Once you know the principles of bringing something into existence and living it, then it doesn't matter what the declaration is. Master one thing, master all things. I'm a good husband, a good dad, because I mastered this football thing. Your kids get the same idea, and then the people who are around you get the same idea, and everyone transforms together. Now, that's a cool life. That's a fun life because now you're surrounded by people you respect and honor, instead of being around a bunch of amateurs going, "I don't even know what we're talking about. What are we doing? I'm confused!" That's what the rest of the world does just to keep themselves safe from risk.

So you can live this really cool life, but it comes with skinned knees and bloody noses. Who cares? You've had them before, you'll have them again as you keep going toward your declaration.

That's what I want for myself, for my family, for my clients: Declare what you are and what you're going to be. Then go live it.

Lauren Holiday Going for Gold, Time After Time

One thing (among many) that I admire about Lauren is her bulldog determination. She decided at the age of five to win an Olympic gold medal, and she never gave up. What happens when you have this single-minded determination is, after a while, the world starts conspiring *with* you. Crazy stuff happens that you can't explain but that helps take you to the next level, again and again. But first, you have to follow that declaration with a focused passion. Then, when you begin to achieve your declaration, you set new ones. You keep your aim right on being the best, whatever that best may be. This is how Lauren did it:

I was cut from the 2008 Olympic team and had to reset my mind to go back to UCLA and train harder than ever. I remember thinking, *I don't ever want to be cut again. This is the worst feeling in the world.*

But the last game before the team went to the send-off game, Abby Wambach went down. My dad was watching the game on TV, and I was in my room packing, and he yelled, "Lauren, Abby's hurt! She's really hurt!"

I was thinking, *Oh, she's dramatic. She's not that hurt.* Fifteen minutes later, my phone rang, and it was Abby. "Chain? I'm 95 percent sure my leg is detached from my body. I don't think I'm supposed to be calling you, but you're going to the Olympics."

"You're crazy; you're just being dramatic," I told her.

"I'm in the ambulance; my leg is broken; you're going to the Olympics." And then she told me loved me and she believed in me, and she wished me good luck.

Thirty minutes later, I got a call from the GM of the national team. "Pack your bags," she told me. "You're going to meet us in San Francisco tomorrow. You're going to the Olympics."

I figured I was going there for moral support, so I decided to be the best cheerleader and the best teammate they had ever seen. After all, there was a chance that I wouldn't even play. So two other teammates and I got the nickname "Team Annoying" because we yelled and screamed and went crazy over everything and had a great time.

I didn't play the first three games, and then one of our girls cramped, and the coach called my name. I played the rest of that game, and I played the quarters and the semis and the finals, and I was first up off the bench in the final game. We won the Olympic gold medal.

That feeling of winning an Olympic gold is indescribable. It's so much bigger than you. Winning a World Cup is amazing, but winning an Olympics . . . it's like you won for Team USA. You represent something so much greater than yourself, so much greater than anything that just has to do with soccer. We represented something that we couldn't even grasp, and that's what's so special about the Olympics.

My [U-21] coach had always told us, "You never want to get too high, and you never want to get too low. Don't let your highest high be winning something; you always have to have something past that to look forward to." I thought of that in China after winning the gold medal. Everyone was celebrating, and we were going to all these events. I kept thinking, *This isn't it. This isn't it. Enjoy it, enjoy every minute, but then go back to work.*

But to be honest, it was hard going back to college soccer after winning. It seemed almost pointless. I knew I had to retrain my mind-set. You don't win an Olympic gold medal and then go back to college and not care. You have to be the best at that level, too. That experience taught me about bouncing back after an emotional high. The first thing I did was set a new goal. This time, I wanted to have a starting position in the Olympics. I didn't want to come in from the bench. It's crazy how your mind switches. Like, "Yes, we won the gold. But now I want to start. I want to be a leader on the team. I want to be someone that they can't not have out there." And that's how my mind-set shifted.

Heading into the 2011 World Cup, I was still not a starter. The day before the start of the event, my teammates and I were together watching the news coverage, and the announcer said, "Lauren Cheney will be starting over Megan Rapinoe in the first game of the World Cup." My coach hadn't even told me! My team and I looked at each other like, *What just happened?*

But Megan was my biggest support, even though I had taken her starting spot. She told me I deserved to be out there and that I should just do my best. It was a real shock, because we played two different positions, and we loved playing together and were always encouraging each other. We had both been competing for a starting position, and then they switched my position to hers, which meant I was playing out of position; the whole thing was completely out of the blue.

At this time, we also played in a professional league. I was in Kansas City, and we won the league, which was of course something else I wanted to do. I had won the Olympics; I was hoping to win the World Cup; we won the league championship. Everything I was accomplishing, I had dreamed of doing.

And that's when I started thinking about my future and thinking about what else I wanted to do. I prayed about it for two years, and I didn't talk to many people about it, besides Jrue. But after we won that league championship, I remember thinking, *Okay, now you need to win a World Cup,* and that was my new goal. I remember going into that World Cup year thinking that I would play one more cycle—a cycle is the World Cup and the Olympics; the Olympics comes the very next year after the World Cup. I prayed and self-evaluated and realized that what I wanted was the World Cup, but even if we didn't win, I would walk away from the game.

I was ready to do something else, to have impact somewhere else. I wanted to start a family. A professional athlete's lifestyle is selfish, I think—not in a way that is abusive of others but selfish in a way that your career and your drive to be the best matter more than anything else. I missed weddings and birthdays, and my friends having babies, and it all affected me more than I realized. That's when I understood that I had accomplished everything I wanted to in soccer. I was ready to move on and be present for my family—be there for a wedding, be with my siblings, and with my husband's family, and not miss out on other people's big things. Even with Jrue playing in the NBA, I felt like our relationship was more about me and my schedule. And I started to feel like I didn't want that anymore. I didn't want it to always be all about me.

Creating "the Best" Declaration

I've committed to a declaration four times, and each one has had the words *the best* in it. *I want to be the best safety in the world. I want to be the best stage performer in the world. I want to be the best playwright. I want to be the best speaker and trainer.* Now, I'm working on a new declaration, something like: *I want to be the best at creating the best, at helping other people become the best.*

What I like about using *the best* in your declaration is that it's specific. You know exactly where you are on the map when you're aiming toward being the best at something.

I was onstage with a brain expert once who said, "You know why you've always been able to reach these goals of yours? It's because you use the term *the best.* Your brain knows exactly what to do with that information. If you said to yourself, 'I want to become an NFL player,' that's a little general. There are a lot of NFL players, but there's only one best safety. When you say you're going to be the best NFL safety, your brain actually goes to work on what it wants. So if a little kid makes a declaration to win an Olympic medal, her brain can interpret that as gold, silver, or bronze. It's kind of iffy. But if you declare you're going to win a gold medal, your brain gets busy with that. You have to be specific."

So let's take the expert's advice and be specific. I want you to declare that you're going to be the best in the world at a thing. I don't care what the thing is. That's up to you to decide. But once you declare it, it radically simplifies your life. All other options are off the table. You know where you are in the world; it's very clear to you. If your declaration is "I'm going to be the best ballerina in the world" or "I'm going to be the best business executive in the world" or "I'm going to be the best pastry chef," it makes things really simple. It's clear when you're *not* the best. And you know the work you have to do. You know where to go.

Keep in mind that once you make this declaration, 99 percent of the time you'll be off course. You'll only be on course 1 percent of the time. That sounds outrageous, right? But it's true. You're distracted here or you've got a vacation there, a family emergency over here, an un-expected deadline—life, in other words. So it helps if you think of yourself as a plane leaving Los Angeles for Maui. What happens on a long flight like that? The pilots take the plane through takeoff and get up to cruising altitude. Then they put the plane on automatic pilot, then they eat their lunch and talk with passengers and do whatever else they do, and the autopilot is guiding that jet all the way to Maui. It's actually off course for almost the entire time, but it keeps correcting itself, and eventually it lands exactly where it's supposed to be.

Think of yourself like that jet. Your job is not to beat yourself up, not to be ashamed of failing to keep your word and your declaration. Your job is to right the ship. Sometimes that correction will be day to day, sometimes hour to hour, and some days it's minute to minute. By using the phrase *the best,* you know when you're off course. It's just a matter of checking in and then making adjustments to get yourself back on course. That action you're taking right now—is it in line with your plan to be the best? Yes? Great. Carry on. No? Course correct now.

The great thing about the declaration is that it takes precedence over everything. You're tired and don't want to get out of bed? You get out of bed and work out because that's what your declaration tells you to do. And you do that for ten, fifteen, twenty years so that your plan has enough time to breathe and to come into existence. Don't make the mistake most people make of giving themselves a short timeline. You need decades to become the best.

This way of living is simple, but it's not easy. Especially at first, it can be pretty tough because you're changing your fundamental way of being. You've declared what you're going to be the best at, and now you're out there trying to do it. You won't get a lot of support from our culture, because everything else in our world is coming at you with mediocrity. But after a while, being the best becomes your natural state of being. You're automatically righting the ship over and over and over again, all the way to Maui, all the way to being the best.

This is not necessarily enjoyable or fun a lot of the time. You're adapting to this new way of being, and you're trying to operate way beyond your comfort zone. You're faced with struggle day in and day out. It can feel really hard.

Just commit to it. Make the declaration and then live it out.

If you've made a true declaration—we'll go over how to do that at the end of this chapter—your life does change. I've walked hundreds of people through this process. Once you make the declaration, and you draw and create and craft your life, you've designed your life of being the best. So if you've declared you're going to be the best ballerina in the world, for instance, your entire life shifts. You start wearing the clothes that the best ballerina in the world wears. You eat the foods that the best ballerina eats. You say the words that the best ballerina says. You start being the best, start really living it out with each choice, every day. And once you start that process, there's only one way that it can't happen. There's one way out, and that is you've got to quit. You have to actually, consciously quit. If you've made a real declaration, then this thing is going to happen, come hell or high water, unless you proactively decide that you're going to pursue mediocrity instead. People do that all the time. They don't consciously declare they're going to be mediocre, but that's what they do. They settle for the scraps.

You're reading this book. You're not that sort of person. You're going to be the best.

Let me tell you a story about the power of a real declaration. In 1969, I drew up my first declaration—that little crayon drawing of me being the best safety in the world. As that plan progressed and I got older, I added onto the dream that I wanted to win the Super Bowl in the twentieth year of my plan.

So here's what happened. In the nineteenth year of that twenty-year plan, I was traded from the Houston Oilers, who weren't going to win the Super Bowl, to the San Francisco 49ers. Now I had a chance to win the Super Bowl. In my plan's twentieth year, 1989, I was right on schedule. But after four games, I got injured, had surgery, and was released from the team. And the team went on to win the Super Bowl that year. They won it without me, but I'm telling you, I know my declaration had something to do with that Super Bowl victory. Part of the power of a true declaration is that you carry everyone along with you. I've played with a huge number of Hall of Fame players, and I believe that other people will get caught up in your declaration, in your story, and they'll go wherever you're headed. Remember my story about my high school football buddies, how four guys from a tiny team with twenty-seven players ended up in the NFL? And how years later my teammates figured that if I could do it, they could do it, too?

That's the power of a true declaration. People might say, "Hey, that's kind of selfish," or, "That's pretty arrogant, to think you could be the best." And I say, "Well, if you follow my declaration and you follow me, you're going to end it with me. You're going to be the best, too."

This declaration has the strongest effect on the people

closest to you. For instance, my son, Axel, has this dream to play both NFL and NBA ball. The other day, a dad asked me, "Bo, how did Axel get so athletic and fast and good at both football and basketball?" And you just know he was thinking it was mostly genetics, right?

"We train a lot," I told him. "You've got to work before school and after school."

This guy was just flabbergasted. He said, "How can the kids work before school? School starts at eight!"

"Well, you know, you've got to get up at five and work."

"Axel gets up at five in the morning? I could never get my kid up at five in the morning."

"Yeah, Axel gets up. I wake him up at five or six or whenever we're working out, and when he opens his eyes, I'm rubbing his back just like my dad used to do for me each morning, and he puts his feet on the floor and he gets up. Not once since he was seven years old has he said, 'You know what, Dad, I just want to sleep in today. Let's skip training this morning.' He's never said that."

I couldn't believe I was telling this other dad that, and he couldn't believe what I was saying. And I think I know why Axel has never once said he didn't want to get out of bed and train. It's because when he was about seven, he saw *Runt of the Litter*. And he saw in the play the ritual of my dad rubbing my back and telling me I was the best, and I would get up and get to work. I think he took that on as his own declaration, except he's going to do it better— he's going to do it in two sports instead of just one.

So right here, you can see how if you have a declaration, you're going to carry along everyone around you. For Axel, my declaration of being the best safety in the NFL, which was made before he was born—made before I even met his mom—that declaration has already changed his life, and he's not even a teenager yet.

I tell a story about my bulletin board in my play, and it's worth repeating here. My dad never watched TV, but one day he was home doing that—a football game. There was a young running back who was about to break the record for the most rushing yards in a single game. My dad was calling my mom to come watch, telling me and my brother to come watch. I could see how happy he was for the kid when he broke the record and his teammates picked him up above their heads and carried him off the field.

The next day in school, all the boys were talking about that kid and how he was their new hero, and how he could run and score touchdowns better than anyone who had ever come before. That kid was O. J. Simpson, the Juice, and I cut his picture out of the sports page and pinned it onto this bulletin board that my aunt had made for me and my brother. She'd put my brother's name at the top and my name down at the bottom. And on each side of our names were these felt animal cutouts. Next to my brother's name was a charging buffalo on one side and a lion on the other. Down at the bottom, near my name, was a bird of some kind—like a pigeon—and on the other side was a kangaroo. I took that picture of O. J. Simpson and I pinned it right over the top of that pigeon. And that was the day I vowed to play pro football. I was nine years old. I'd never seen a game before that day, I'd never even touched a football, but that day I made a promise—my declaration—that I would one day play pro football.

I didn't care about running with the ball. What struck me about the picture I cut out were the guys hanging on to O.J. trying to bring him down. I wanted to be one of those guys. All the boys at my school wanted to be O.J. Not me. I wanted to stop him. Everyone else wanted to score touchdowns. I wanted to win. I wanted to take control of the game. And to control this game, you have to play defense. Because if they can't score, they can't win.

I noticed that there's one position on the defense that single-handedly decides the outcome of every football game—the safety. There's nothing safe about that position. You have to run forward, sideways, and backward faster than the fastest man in the world runs forward. And there's nobody back there. Nobody. The safety is the last line of defense. If you get past the safety, you score, and if you score, you win.

If you can't get past me, you lose. It's that simple. The safety decides who wins and who loses. It's a decision. It's about desire.

So I stole my sister's crayons, and I architected this plan. I had fifteen years to go until I would graduate from college and be eligible for the NFL draft. That gave me fifteen years to become the best safety in the world and then five years after that to win the Super Bowl. That was how the twenty-year plan started. That was my declaration.

What I didn't know then and what I know now is that when you make a declaration like that, you have to back it up by creating an intimate and profound relationship with your future self.

Here's what I mean by that. Back when I was a little kid drawing out my twenty-year plan using my sister's crayons, what I was really doing was seeing myself as I would be twenty years in the future. I saw myself as the best safety in the world even though I wasn't. I was a little kid! But that vision of my future self changed everything about me on a daily basis. I walked like the best safety, I talked like the best safety, I ate like the best safety, I trained like the best safety until I actually was the best safety.

When I was in high school, I put a picture of Walter Payton in my locker. He was one of the greatest running backs ever to play the game, and I loved watching him play. And I wanted to take him down. I wanted to stop him. So for four years of high school, ten times a day when I opened my locker, there was Walter Payton looking right at me. He had all his pads and his helmet on, and he was running right at the camera with the football in his hand.

That's the picture I looked at ten times a day for four years.

Cut to 1985. I was in my second year with the Houston Oilers. We were playing against the Chicago Bears.

Their running back was Walter Payton, and I was playing safety. They gave him the ball, and I was running up
to tackle him, and suddenly my whole life turned into
slow motion. I was looking at Walter Payton and he was
looking at me, and we were about to make a collision. It
was the exact same picture that was in my locker. He dis-
played the same body language. He was looking right
into the camera, which was me now. I only had to do one
thing: tackle him. I remember thinking, *Oh my God, I'm
about to tackle Walter Payton, the guy I've been looking
at all these years.* Sure enough, I took him right down to
the ground, and I couldn't believe it.

Here's a thing I found out. Great players like Walter
Payton do not want rookies lying on top of them. I was
so shocked I'd tackled him that I was just lying on top of
him thinking, *Oh, shit, I hope Mom and Dad saw that
on TV! I just tackled Walter Payton!* So instead of getting off him, I was lying on him, kind of relishing the
moment, and Walter Payton pushed me off him and then
kicked me in the private parts. He dropped some language
on me, and I realized, *Okay, this is serious. No more hero
worship.*

But that picture in my locker? That relationship with
my future self? I actually lived that out. That came into
fruition.

Here's another one. My senior year in high school, I
hung up a picture of a guy named Mike Reinfeldt. At that
time, 1979, he was the most valuable defensive player in

the NFL. He was a free safety for the Houston Oilers. I loved Mike Reinfeldt. I wanted to *be* Mike Reinfeldt.

Fast-forward to 1984 when I was drafted as a free safety to Houston. Guess who their free safety was when I got there? Mike Reinfeldt. I was competing for a job with the guy I had been staring at for all those years. He was one of the nicest guys I'd ever met, and he taught me everything he knew. Houston drafted me to replace my hero, and I did. I'll never forget watching him pack up eight years of football shoes and equipment out of his locker, which was right next to mine, and I remember feeling sad about it, watching him walk out of that locker room. But I'd seen my future, and I'd rehearsed for it, and it had came to fruition.

That's why I have our kids cut out pictures of their heroes and put them on boards and look at them every day. I tell them, "You're going to have to defeat your heroes, and when you do, that is a weird day." And kids will say stuff like, "Oh, he's so great, she's so great, I could never be like that." And I just keep saying, "You actually will be like that. You're going to have to go nose to nose with your heroes because that's how it comes true."

That stuff works. I've done it over and over and over again. It works. People won't do it because they don't believe they can actually be or defeat their hero. But that's part of being the best in the world at something.

I want you to think about your declaration as being similar to the Declaration of Independence. That document is nearly 250 years old, and yet we live out that declaration every day. That declaration stays alive because we are keeping it alive.

If you really want to be the best, the relationship with who you are in the future has to be intimate. And it has to start today. You have to write it out, draw it out (even if you think you're a lousy artist), and then live it into being. My imagination put it on the page, and then I lived it out over and over until it became real.

Living according to your declaration is simpler than having a list of actions that you have to take, because it's a way of being. It's a way of living. You *be like* the best and you end up being the best. People say to me, "You always want to be the best, and that's really hard." My response always is, "If you think being the best is hard, try being mediocre. That's really hard because we're not made that way. You won the first race you entered. Your nature is to be great."

If I see somebody is great and I speak them into their own greatness, and they push back against that and argue against their own greatness, that person is going to have a really hard time becoming great. It's going to be impossible until and unless they change the way they believe and see things. I've had to do that with people—tell them that it's okay to be the best. They may have been told when they were growing up that it wasn't okay to think of themselves as the best or to give themselves that high goal to aim at. But their lives can transform and take off if they get permission from someone to actually live into their greatness.

So that's what I'm doing right now. I'm giving you permission to live into your innate greatness. Let's start by creating your declaration.

ACTION STEP: YOUR DECLARATION AND YOUR LETTER

Here's where you name it—that space where you're the best. Do you want to be the best business executive? The best pop singer? The fastest runner? The top-selling mystery writer? You name it; you claim it; you point your life toward it. This is your vision. This is your life.

Think of your declaration as being the key to the car of everything. You're now in control of your destiny. Where can this thing go? You're no longer on a fixed path determined by your genetics, your position in life, what other people tell you is possible, or what you've done up until now. That's all out the window as far as I'm concerned. You're creating your own reality. You're creating what's impossible and making it possible. You're building your own road.

Now write down your declaration in words. One or two sentences will do. Plain, straightforward language works best; this is not a corporate mission statement. It's a simple "I'm going to be the best." That's what you should be writing.

Now draw it. Don't tell me you can't draw. I'm not interested in what you can't do. This declaration needs words, and it needs pictures. My first declaration—the one written in crayon—showed me in a football uniform.

My most recent one showed me on a stage, speaking and teaching. I can't draw. It doesn't matter. You need the pictures. Your brain needs the visual to back up the written words. You've created your future knowing that it's going to happen. So get comfortable with what it's going to look like.

This declaration is your all-attractive piece. It's where you're going to be spending your days. Your time and all your decisions will be based on that declaration. *Yes* and *no* are all based on that declaration. If you're asked to do something that's not in line with your declaration, you're going to say no. If it's in line with your declaration, if it moves you closer to your future self, you say yes.

You'll discover pretty quickly that living by your declaration, being the best, is all about eliminating things. It's not about adding things. Your path is clear because you say no to anything that takes you away from your goal. You're course-correcting most of the time, remember?

Once you've written and drawn your declaration, write me a letter. Date it twenty years into the future, and your declaration has been achieved. Now tell me in this letter about all the obstacles you overcame along the way. All the heartache you faced. All the sweat and blood and tears you left on your path.

The reason we do this is because, as I've already mentioned, the person with the most intimate and profound relationship with their future self is the most successful. I want you making today's decisions based on your relationship with your future self.

If you name the obstacles you're going to circumvent, those obstacles aren't so monstrous. You named them, you created them, they're of your making, and you're the one who can go past them. But if obstacles are just the big boogeyman, not really defined but just sort of looming, they carry a lot of weight. They take up a lot of what-if space in your brain. They stop you from ever fully committing.

And if you've truly committed, believe me, you've just guaranteed yourself a bunch of obstacles. That's great! The fun part of life is fighting through those obstacles. Also, I can promise you that if you don't have an enemy to put your nose up against, no one will pay attention to you. The only thing human beings are interested in is struggle and how we overcome it. If you don't have struggles, people will dismiss you immediately. You're unwatchable. It's like watching a noncompetitive sport. There's no attraction to the viewer or to the player because there's nothing at stake.

Go to boeason.com/actionsteps for your Declaration Worksheet and examples of powerful letters and declarations.

4.

PREPARATION

Usain Bolt has won nine gold medals. Every time that guy stepped on a track, you just knew he was going to leave everyone else in the dust for those 100-meter sprints. He ran for less than two minutes total—115 seconds—in three Olympics, and he made $119 million in endorsements. That's more than $1 million for every second.

But here's the thing. He trained for twenty years for those two minutes of Olympic competition. It's not like he was born running fast. He trained and trained and trained. Most people just see the time on the track, the 115 seconds. I see the miles he ran to get there.

That's what we're talking about in this chapter—preparation. To be the best, you need to completely flip the culture's relationship to practice and performance. Practice has to be the center of your universe. And because you're going to be practicing outside your current capacity, it's hard to pull this off consistently. You can't phone it in. That's not how you improve. It's not easy. But if it were easy, everyone would do it. It's not about being easy. It's not about enjoyment. It's not about having a good time. It's about greatness. And you absolutely must be out of your comfort zone to adapt to the new level and to achieve greatness.

So if our intent is to be the best in the world at a thing in twenty years, what do we have to resolve? What do we have to put to bed? What never has to be an issue for us again? It's just plain hard work. And no one wants to talk about those years, those ten or fifteen or twenty years of hard work that you're facing, because it's just uncomfortable.

I'm not going to lie. Some days you're going to go backward. The only thing that matters is that you stay outside your comfort zone and you keep challenging homeostasis. You keep committing. It's where your greatness lives.

Daniel Coyle, who wrote *The Talent Code,* studied several hotbeds of talent around the world—tennis clubs, swim centers, classical music schools, dance academies— and he found that successful people don't practice more, and they don't practice harder. They don't have more discipline than other people, and they weren't born bigger, stronger, or more talented in any way. What they do have that's different from the general population is a completely different relationship to practice.

So let's think about that for a minute. All of us who make a true declaration have to change our relationship to practice. To most people, probably even you at this point, practice or rehearsal sounds like when you tell kids they have to eat their vegetables. It's drudgery. It's dread. It's something to get out of or to do as little as possible. But people in those hotbeds of talent, people who end up being the best in the world? They love practice. They show up for it enthusiastically. Practice is the center of their universe.

As Daniel Coyle says in his book, "For them, practice *is* the big game."

Everyone else thinks the big game is the big game, but it never is. You do not get paid as an athlete for the game; you don't get paid as a writer for the story. You get paid for the practice or the rehearsal or the training that led you to that performance. So we have to totally shift our relationship to practice. For the rest of the world, performance is 90 percent of their time, and the practice backing it up was about 10 percent of their time. That has to be flipped.

From here on out, the center of your universe is rehearsal, is practice, is training. Your life is going to be 90 percent of your time preparing for your performance, which will be 10 percent of your time.

Struggle is a biological necessity to us. You should attempt to fail more than everybody else, because that means you're trying harder than anyone else. And eventually you get so good at it that you're the best. And that's no accident. That's because of practice. I mean, this shit doesn't fall off trees. You have to practice outside your comfort zone all the time.

I trained for years to put on my play, *Runt of the Litter*. Long before that play ever hit a stage, I was training for it—writing it, rewriting it, working with movement and voice coaches. Then, before each performance, I had four hours of warm-up. The play itself lasts about ninety minutes onstage.

Remember: 90 percent practice, 10 percent performance. That's your new world.

Sometimes my kids will say, "Dad, that's not fun." Yeah, you know what? Being the best is fun. Getting to that level of being the best is *not* fun. But it's an honorable way to live.

I've been on other people's stages and talked about this stuff. The host will often come up to me after I'm done and go, "Shit, Bo, you can't say that stuff. You say the words *hard work* and *struggle*. You just said that to my audience. You can't say that stuff to my audience. They don't like those words. We pulled them out of all our presentations."

And I'm like, "Really? Am I supposed to lie to them and tell them they don't have to do anything? They just have to show up? Because that does not work."

This is what I'm talking about when I discuss going counter to the culture. You're facing this headwind, this pushback, because we're programmed to believe we can make a lot of money from doing nothing. That we are entitled to certain things. And that we don't have to do anything for what we get. We don't have to earn it. We just get it delivered to us.

So if that's how you've been thinking, my way of doing things is a huge shift. You have to build up the fortitude it takes to be the best in the world at this thing. It's an uphill climb the whole way. And it looks like it's never going to happen. The whole entire time you're working toward this declaration, it looks like it isn't going to happen.

But I've done this four times, and it happens every time. Even when it seems completely impossible, that it can't happen, it happens.

So I'm sure a lot of you right now are thinking, *Why am I even reading this? Shoot, really? This is nuts.* You're thinking of the years and the tears and the rocky road. You're asking yourself, *Why didn't I just grab a book where somebody talks about ease and luxury? Where someone is telling me, "Hey, make a million dollars in one weekend! It's easy. I'll teach you how."* Well, this is not my experience. I don't find that to be true. Nothing truly great ever happened in the history of the world without hard work.

So that's the good news, and it's also the bad news. No one else is going to work that hard, so you've got no competition. Great news, right? But the bad news is this book is not going to tell you how to make a million bucks in a weekend without doing any work. That's not how I work; that's not how the world works; that's not what I'm teaching you here.

You have to prepare to be great, so buckle in. You're making a decades-long commitment.

Keep in mind that it's not easy or indifferent practice you'll be engaging in. It's deliberate practice. It's practice that's outside your comfort zone. So that means it will be a struggle. It will be unenjoyable a lot of the time. And that's where people quit. Most people don't like to struggle, so they never get any better. But as human beings, we have the ability to learn and to get better at things. We know how to adapt to our circumstances. We just don't want to put the work in, because we'd rather lie around being comfortable.

Most people won't commit to going through the struggle, so they will never get better. They'll for sure never be the best. And if you don't do deliberate practice—practice outside your current capacity, outside your comfort zone—then your body never has to adapt to anything. It gets soft and lazy. You're never challenging yourself.

Understand that you are walking away from that life right now. You are now in the business of getting better, because you're attempting to be the best, and I'm right here with you. We're going to live beyond our current capacity every single day. We're going to struggle. You might not want to hear this, but the struggle does not end. It's not like you get to a certain level and graduate and it's all over. Greatness doesn't live like that. Every time you think you've gotten to the top, you just put yourself at the bottom of the next mountain and start climbing that new mountain. All these summits that you think you're going to achieve are actually false summits. You're satisfied for two seconds, and then you're on to the next climb.

Joan Rosenberg, Ph.D.

I've known Joan for years and saw how quickly she caught on to the principles I teach. In fact, as a psychologist, master clinician, trainer, and consultant, she has attended many of my events to help attendees deal with any emotional or psychological issues that may arise. This is what Joan had to say about helping to prepare yourself for the journey of becoming the best:

Most people are encouraged to do their best and try new things as they grow up. But at the same time, they're often discouraged from standing out. So people can have a really hard time differentiating between this notion of desiring to be the best, or actually being the best, and also managing that without looking conceited to others. However, I typically find that when someone is playing at the top of their game, they have no need to insist that other people see them in that light. Look at Bo. There's nothing flashy there. It's just him showing up as who he is in the world.

Bo centers everything on the idea that being the best is, in essence, your birthright. What that does, particularly for adults, is open that space again. It gives the kid over twenty the permission they had when they were younger to go after what they desire. It opens up a permission within ourselves, sort of "I want that, I've already desired that, I've yearned for that, and now I feel like I have external permission to go after it again."

After so many years of not going after what they

dreamed about, people often have difficulty making the decision to take that first step in the years-long journey of becoming the best. You don't have control over how the process evolves, but you do have control over your commitment to it.

Bo talks about the necessity for deliberate practice, and I would add that we need two other things. We need ongoing and constructive feedback from a coach or a mentor or supervisor, and we need self-reflection. We need to take the time to think through, *That didn't work out so well. What can I do to improve on it?* or *What about that was successful? I should repeat it.* Ideally, you build on your experience; you build on figuring out what to improve and what to repeat.

You also must have the willingness to be vulnerable, which I define as an openness and willingness to be hurt and to learn. You must also be able to handle the unpleasant feelings, the disappointment, that will come up as you take this long journey.

And I make a distinction between disappointment and rejection. If you say, "He rejected me," the center of power is in that other person, and you can do nothing about it. But if you define rejection as disappointment, well, you just didn't get the outcome you wanted. So you may have anger or some other hurt feelings about that outcome, but those feelings can be short-lived.

Again, when you understand that you are committed to the journey, you'll experience those feelings as just part of that journey. So you anticipate that you'll get upset along the way, and also that it is up to you to manage your emotional state. When you categorize "rejection" as "disappointment" or "embarrassment" or "anger" or "sadness," then you retain the power to manage those emotions. There is much growth in that.

My new book, *90 Seconds to a Life You Love*, explains how to master your difficult feelings and cultivate long-lasting confidence, resilience, and authenticity. If people don't allow themselves to move through the feelings— embarrassment, disappointment, whatever they might be—then they're not able to get the insights that come from actually experiencing the feeling. They shut down on opportunities for insight.

To be truly great, it's about starting and not stopping. You make the declaration, and then you commit to *I'm doing this, and it doesn't matter what I go through; I'm staying the course.* That's the same mentality we adopt when we work with Bo and make a declaration. No matter what we face, we hold a no-brainer, this-is-done, I'm-in-it attitude. I don't know where this will take me. I don't know how I'm getting there. I don't even need to know how I'm going to get there. I just know that I shoot for the end goal: Here's my outline of what I think might happen, and now I'm going for it.

With that mind-set, you actually build in the anticipation that you'll hit those obstacles. And then once you hit an obstacle, you don't let the devastation or embarrassment or sadness stop you. You just experience it and sit with the authentic truth of that experience. And then ask yourself, *Am I staying or stopping? Is this goal important enough for me to stay the course even though I know I'm going to hit more obstacles?* Then you reframe your belief about the disappointment. That's where you turn the obstacle into an opportunity for growth and learning. And then you just get back up and recommit, every day, just like Bo does.

The "Never Do Again" List

So how are you going to get there? You're crazy busy right now. You can't possibly add anything else to your daily, weekly, monthly to-do lists. You have family and career and community obligations. Where are you going to find the time to practice and then practice some more and then practice some more?

You don't have to find extra time, because to fulfill this declaration you made, you've got to eliminate stuff. And that opens up all sorts of time.

I know you're thinking, *Bo, there's no way I can eliminate anything. I have responsibilities and commitments!* Stay with me on this, though. I do an exercise with my group called "List Your Distractions." It's an amazing thing to do because it shows people where they're wasting time. Watching TV, scrolling through social media websites, shopping, binge eating, the list goes on.

So I have people make their distractions list, and then, working from that list, they make their "Never Do Again" list. This is just what it sounds like. It's the list of things you're never going to do again, or do as little as possible. For me, a few years ago I realized I just don't like being on the phone. And so I put that on my list: I'm never going to be on the phone. Now I'm on the phone only sometimes, and when I am, it's of my own doing. It's phone calls that I want to have. I'm not at the beck and call of anybody who wants to talk to me.

The thing about the "Never Do Again" list is that you don't have to make it happen all at once. It's like a declaration. Write out your list, and the things on it will gradually fall away over the course of months or years. Eating certain foods or eating in certain ways, watching the news, wasting huge chunks of time on Facebook, going to parties you really don't want to attend, all that stuff just drops away.

What happens when you make the list is that you're left with the things you actually *will* do. So this is a very cool exercise to see how resistant you are to stepping into your own greatness. It also shows you exactly what you have to commit to in order to never do those things again. This one exercise alone can make your life stunningly simple.

A lot of people get stuck thinking about everything they won't get to do anymore. And that's true. It's important to acknowledge this. Things will be going away from your life, things you're comfortable with and used to—your distractions list. But you also get to say no to the things that don't line up with you being the best. There's something incredibly powerful about that. You're going to enjoy it and be surprised at how good it feels.

What you'll recognize as you get further into this process is that right now, you're committed to false loyalties. We all are. We go to gatherings because we think we're supposed to show up. We're nice to someone we dislike because we think we're supposed to be. We attend a meeting because we feel obligated. We watch a TV show or a sports event because everyone else is watching it and we want to fit in. But if that meeting or those people or parties don't line up with you being the best, then they can be eliminated from your schedule. And that really streamlines your life.

I like that streamlined life. I remember when I was in the NFL, how everything else just fell away. The bosses get you from the hotel to the stadium on a team bus, and the stadium parking lot is filled with people celebrating, barbecuing, drinking beer, painting themselves, putting tattoos on, wearing costumes. So they're all celebrating, and you're on this bus, not celebrating anything. You're nervous. And when you pull into the parking lot, they come charging up to the bus, and they're pounding on the bus and waving at you—or if you're the opposing team, they're throwing stuff at the bus and spitting on it and flipping you off.

As a player, I always felt weird about that. I've trained my whole life to be on this bus, but they're the ones out there celebrating. They're the ones eating hot dogs and drinking beer. I had to eat a healthy breakfast, and now I'm having this nutritious pregame drink instead of a beer. But they're here to see me, and they're basically paying to see those twenty years of training I put in.

I saw them every week, and it seemed they were envious of me because I'm on this team and I'm going to go play this game. And I was envious of them because they were having a great time and I wasn't. So that's part of being the best: the loss of that casual, carefree celebration that fans have but players don't.

This isn't true of all players, but it was how I lived. I remember deciding not to go to my high school prom because I thought going to the prom was not equal to getting into the NFL. I almost never drank beer. I missed parties that my friends went to. I saw all those things as options, and I felt like I had a psychological edge by not doing those things. So for me, when I chose my option and made my declaration, I suffered loss because of the elimination of all those other things.

And people don't see that. They don't see what successful people have left behind on their way to the top. When I was rehearsing for my play, I ran into Mikhail Baryshnikov in the elevator several times because his dance studio was in that same building. And the first time I met him, I was just overwhelmed, thinking, *Oh my God, this is the greatest dancer in history. He totally changed that art form.* And then I looked down at his feet and saw he was barefoot. He was barefoot because his feet are totally mangled. And just like that, I didn't see Baryshnikov; I saw the miles and the hours and the decades it took him to be the best. I saw what it took for him to change the art form. His feet tell that story.

When I see Baryshnikov dance or hear Yo-Yo Ma play

the cello or watch Usain Bolt run, I think of what they had to give up to be able to do that. All I see is the work they put in and the years of loss. But I'm the one paying to see them, and they're the ones on the stage.

The hardest thing about being the best is that you have to be reminded that that's what you signed up for. You signed up to run those miles. You signed up for constant deliberate practice. You signed up to stop taking the easy way out and to challenge yourself every single day. You signed up to get those mangled feet.

Remember, there is no Plan B. And once you've closed all those doors and shut down every exit, you have a huge amount of power.

Years ago, one of my mentors asked me, "Bo, who do you think has the most power in a prison?" And of course, I'd never even considered that question. I said, "I don't know. The warden? The guards?"

"No, the warden doesn't have any power, and the guards don't have any power, and the people who are getting out of prison don't have any power. All the power in a prison belongs to the lifers. Because they have that lifetime sentence. They've heard the cell doors close. They know they're never leaving. So they put down stakes. They decorate their cell. They move in, and they take over. The temporary prisoners don't put down roots, because they're counting the days until they get out. So they hold no power. Only the lifers do. And you can get really creative, use all your power, and make all your dreams come true because you are starting from a point of never leaving."

He told me that marriage is the same way. Some people enter marriage thinking in some little molecule somewhere in their body that one day, that jail cell is going to open up. Those are always unsuccessful marriages, because that person is keeping open the possibility that one day, they might leave. The most successful marriages are the ones where the people are lifers. They know they're never leaving. And so they live from that truth. They're lifers.

Players Only Beyond This Point

The most vivid memory I have of playing in the NFL isn't playing against Joe Montana or Walter Payton. My most vivid memory is of a sign. The sign was on our locker room door, and it said, "Absolutely no admittance. Players only beyond this point." The president of the United States could not come in that locker room. The richest person in the world could not come in that locker room. The biggest celebrities on the planet could not come in that locker room. The only way you could enter was if you were a player.

Now, when you enter an event that I'm doing, you are faced with those words. "Players only beyond this point." It's a reminder that we're creating players. You're going to leave my event with a player mentality. And that means your life will shift in ways you cannot imagine. From this day forward, you are no longer a spectator. You are no longer a fan. You are a player. Players play. They don't critique, and they don't have commentary. They play.

I remember several years ago when Peyton Manning was quarterbacking the Denver Broncos in the Super Bowl. He'd been rivals with Tom Brady his whole career, and they battled each other and competed with each other for years. Someone asked Tom Brady, whose team, the New England Patriots, was not going to the Super Bowl that year, if he was going to be watching his rival in the Super Bowl. And Brady said no, he wouldn't be watching.

People went crazy. "Tom Brady's got sour grapes." "Tom Brady is jealous of Peyton Manning." "Tom Brady's not a real football fan."

That's crap. Of course Tom Brady's not a football fan. He is a football *player.* And the Super Bowl was not created for players; it was created for fans. It was created for people who want to watch and party and bet on the outcome. It was created for people who want to watch crazy TV commercials and big flashy halftime shows. It was not created for the people who actually play the game.

This is why when people ask me, "My kid wants to be a pro athlete, Bo. What's the first thing I should do?" I always say, "Turn off sports television. Sports television is not for athletes. It's for fans of athletes. Your kid doesn't want to be a fan, right? So turn the TV off."

Here's an example of the power that comes with thinking of yourself as a player and not a fan. Axel's quarterback coaches also coach Matt Ryan, who took the Atlanta Falcons to the 2017 Super Bowl. A couple of months after that game, Axel's coaches said to me, "Hey, Bo, would

Axel like to come down and train alongside Matt Ryan? We're going to be training him next week." And of course, I said, "Heck, yeah, he'll be there." I took Axel out of school for the day, and we drove down to Orange County to train alongside Matt Ryan.

This was about six weeks after we'd watched Ryan play in the Super Bowl, and I lectured Axel during the entire hour-and-a-half drive. "Even though you're only nine, you're a player, not a fan. A fan would run up to Matt Ryan and get his picture, get an autograph, take a selfie. You're not going to do any of that. You're a player. You're going to be a peer of Matt Ryan's. So you shake his hand, you treat him with respect, and you train alongside him."

We got there, and as soon as I met Matt Ryan, I started turning into a total fanboy! I thought, *Oh, this guy is great! He's a big, strong, terrific leader, as nice as could be, exactly what you'd expect from a quarterback who's led his team to the Super Bowl.* Matt has humility and a wry sense of humor, and he's really gracious and extremely hardworking.

So Axel trained alongside Matt Ryan for the next two hours. Axel worked his butt off, doing everything that Matt Ryan was doing, except he was doing it with a nine-year-old body. And at the end of the training, Ryan ran over to me and Axel. He shook Axel's hand and said, "Man, I love how hard you worked out there. I can't wait to see you in the future. It was really an honor for me to train with you."

We stood there, and I could see that Axel really wanted to ask for his autograph or a picture with him or something like that. And I'd lectured him for ninety minutes about being a player, not a fan, right? Axel and I just had this moment of silence.

And then Matt said, "Hey, anybody got a camera around here?"

I said, "Well, yeah, I have one right here in my pocket," and I hauled out my phone.

He said, "I want to get a picture with this kid, because someday we're going to have to play against each other, and I want to have a picture of when we first started."

So you see what happened there? Axel maintained his player mentality, his peer status, throughout that whole practice, even when I started fanboying on Matt Ryan, and then Ryan took the lead and asked for a picture.

Now, I can't know what Matt Ryan was thinking, but here's how it came across: *This kid worked his ass off. He didn't ask for a picture. He didn't ask for an autograph. He's acting like he's a peer, and I'm going to treat him like one.*

You are not a fan. You are a player only. You are going to be a peer of your heroes, and you have to act like it starting right now.

Players only beyond this point.

Does it sound like hard work? Good, because it is. Don't try to fool yourself that this will be easy. It won't be. It's years of hard work if you're doing it correctly.

But players don't complain. Does that sound like your

life right now? Probably not. People complain about this; they complain about that. Well, as a player, you don't have time to complain. You have time to practice, and you have time to perform. Every complaint is turned into training. Let's say you've got a game scheduled for tonight, and there's going to be a rainstorm during the game. Are they going to cancel that game? No. If there's a blizzard? No. Do they ever cancel the game? Hardly ever. The game is scheduled, and it has to be played. So it's not like players get to vote on whether to play or not. You're playing. The game is on. Get out there and deliver on all those hours and years you spent practicing.

Bring that new reality into your own life now. You might be thinking, *Oh, crap, it's really hot out today, so I'm not doing this,* but you know what? Players play. It's what they do. You don't think about it. You just get out there and play. You need to totally shift your relationship with your own life.

I get how scary that is. We're talking about a major, long-term life change. It's much easier to just stay in your comfort zone, to stay in homeostasis and not try to change anything. It's easier *not* to play. What if you try and fail? What if people don't support you? What if they walk away from you because they don't understand what you're trying to accomplish? There will be people like that. You're probably related to some of them. Some of them might even live in your own home. And that's totally understandable, because our culture is a fan culture, not a player culture. Most people are more interested in pretend activities like managing their fantasy football team than in putting in the hard work to live a better life.

You're going to walk away from a lot of what you know.

But it's worth it. It makes your life more focused and more satisfying. And it actually gets you more time. Your life becomes really simple because you're only going to focus on that one thing, and you're only going to do things that are in line with you being the best at this thing you've declared. That's it. You don't do anything else. Obviously, you aren't going to walk away from your family and work commitments, but you are going to adjust them to the extent that you can. And then you're going to eliminate everything else that doesn't drive you toward your declaration's promise.

Flip Your Struggle, Flip Your Story: Scott Mann's Story

Scott Mann, Lieutenant Colonel (ret.), is a former Green Beret who saw many years of active service overseas. Now he's a speaker and coach, but the path wasn't easy. Here's his story in his own words:

Nothing in my nearly twenty years of Green Beret service prepared me to come back to civilian life. At least, that's what I thought before I met Bo.

People often mix up Green Berets and Navy SEALs. We couldn't be more different, though. SEALs go in on tactical missions, get their job done, and get out. But as part of the U.S. Army Special Forces, also known as the Green Berets, I spent months, years sometimes, working behind enemy lines, forging relationships and connections with the indigenous people in Afghanistan and Colombia. We lived in unbelievably rough places—ask yourself if you could live in a neighborhood that had been under attack for thirty years—and yet were able to gain the trust and support of some incredibly strong people.

While in Afghanistan, we implemented a strategy I call *leading from the rooftop.* This was around 2010, and we were in these little villages that were being attacked by the Taliban. The villagers would not go up onto their rooftops to defend themselves. So we would go up there and defend their villages, then in the mornings, we'd carry our casualties down the ladders from the rooftops, and the villagers would just kind of watch us as we were limping off. They were too terrified of the Taliban to fight back. But we noticed, after a few weeks, that you'd be up on a rooftop and over there on your left would be an old farmer with a rifle, defending his village. Couple of days later, there'd be three, five, ten people up there. Pretty soon the whole village would be defending itself. We did this in 113 villages across the country over the course of eighteen months. We were literally leading from the rooftop. We inspired people to follow us not because they had to but because they chose to. We built leadership by example and by connection. We had to have the courage to climb the ladder by ourselves in the beginning, knowing that eventually people would choose to follow us.

After two decades in the army, I retired. And like a lot of veterans, I had trouble transitioning to civilian life. When you live on the edge every single day, so-called normal life can be exceedingly difficult. My story, my loss, went so deep inside me that I couldn't talk about it. When I first came home, I viewed the struggle the same way every veteran does—you just bear it in silence. There's a reason Special Forces are called *the Quiet Professionals*. Even though I knew instinctively that I needed to speak out, when I looked out across the horizon, there was no example of how to do things differently.

Fortunately, I attended an event at which Bo was one of the speakers. He told his story, and when he talked about breaking his knee and thinking, *I'm gonna go to prison if I don't figure out something else to do*, I knew I had to work with him. I thought my military experience was not applicable to the civilian world, but when I located myself in Bo's story, I realized I could create a different path for myself from the frustrating one I was on. I pulled him aside after the event and told him I wanted to work with him. We worked together for several years, and things started to fall into place for me.

Working with Bo, I learned not just how but *why* to tell my story. I talked about my struggles, my losses, the deaths of twenty-three of my friends in combat situations, the stress of being under fire, and I pretty much just fell apart every single time I talked about it.

So imagine how I felt when Bo told me I would need

to get comfortable with saying the names of all my fallen comrades. Onstage. Out loud. In front of people. I fought against that idea so hard.

"I can't do that!" I protested.

"Dude, you're so lucky. You have to do that," he said.

Lucky? Now I was pissed off.

"You're going to help so many people with your story and your struggle," Bo went on. "You have got to stand there onstage and say each person's name out loud. You have to talk about what you went through with generosity so that other people can connect with you. Change how you view your struggle. Instead of protecting yourself from what you think is going to be more pain, just share the story in the service of others. There are enough people giving us the selfie version, the 'everything is okay' version. Give them the real thing. Do it for yourself, if not for them. It will change your life."

I must have still looked pissed off, because Bo went on, "Look, I worked with a mentor many years ago, and one day he said to me, 'If your knee could talk, what would it say to you right now?' and I just fell on the floor crying. You need to name and give voice to this pain, just like I needed to with mine.

"Flip your struggle; flip your story. Let it be rocket fuel. Let it be what drives you. Talk about it so that people can relate to you as a real person who's been through the struggle, so they can locate themselves in your story."

I trusted Bo, so I decided to let go and embrace that struggle as the epicenter of my story, instead of protecting myself from the pain of reliving the struggle. "It's already done," Bo pointed out. "It can't hurt you anymore."

Eventually, I got comfortable with telling my story. I transformed from a former warrior into a warrior storyteller. I knew that was the movement I wanted to rebuild here at home, because right now there's so much distrust in our country. And that's what I do now. I teach returning veterans, corporate leaders, and heads of nonprofits. I'm a warrior storyteller and a rooftop leader. My nonprofit trains vets in what we call the Hero's Journey—we help them tell their story and find their voice. We aim for transformation like the one I experienced.

The work I've done with Bo has opened up so many opportunities for me, including going national on CNN. I give a storytelling rendition, a narrative, whereas other experts are just talking heads. People crave a story to connect with. And apparently everything I did as a Green Beret was preparation for this phase of my life— connecting with people—and by telling my own story, helping them find their voices and tell their own stories.

To sum it up, I can either own my story . . . or my story is going to own me. Or as we said in the military, "Wannabes admire the problem. Green Berets attack it."

Okay, Bo, How Do I Do This?

Whenever we get to this point in my event, someone always asks, "How? How am I going to do this?" I guarantee you, I have never asked that question, at least not the way most people ask it. I'll bet Al Pacino never asked that question and Mikhail Baryshnikov never asked that question. "How?" is almost always a losing question. When you ask it, you're not looking for a plan. You're looking for a way out; you're saying you can't do it; you're saying you don't really want to do it. You ask, "How?" and you're looking for an excuse. "How?" is one small step away from saying, "I can't. This is impossible. There's no way."

So we have to get rid of this. I know people love knowing how, and I'm going to show you a real way to ask and answer "How?" later in the book. But be aware that when people ask, "How?" what they're almost always saying is "I'm not going to do that because it's too hard" or "I can't do that" or "I don't have what it takes." They don't believe in themselves. They think their goal is impossible or too much work. That's what they really mean when they ask, "How?"

Now, what if you're thinking, *I don't have twenty years to do this,* are you telling me you're not going to be around in twenty years? Well, those twenty years are coming for all of us. I'm going to be nearly eighty years old in twenty years. You can bet I'm going to spend those twenty years getting to be the best at something instead of phoning it in and whining.

Here's another thing: It won't take you twenty years to be successful. You'll have success along the way; you'll make money; you'll change your life. But you need that long time span to become the best, to fulfill your declaration. And it doesn't need to be something new. It could be something you're currently doing—let's say you want to be the best parent, or the best accountant, or the best spouse, or something else you're doing now but you want to be the best. Just name your intention and then get after it.

This is how we want to be, after all. This is our true nature. It's when we get in the way of our true nature, our competitive self, that we get in trouble. When I work with people, whenever they name places where they're letting their instincts work or going with Mother Nature or using their intuition, whatever you want to call it, that's the area of their lives that's going well. Those are the places where they're successful. That's where they shine. And then the places where they're going against their nature, or their internal truth, that's where they have trouble. They run up against brick walls. Nothing seems to go right.

Can you name the places in your life where you are true and loyal to your nature? Those are probably the areas where you have the most peace and the most success. And now if you name the areas in your life where you're going against yourself, you're probably not as successful there, are you? In the first instance, you have freedom. In the second, you've given up your freedom to do something you feel obligated to do; you're never going to be as happy and successful in that area.

Let's go back to that fantasy sports team example again. I don't want you doing things that are fantasy. I want you doing things that are your real, true, gut-level dreams; things that live in the real world, that are active, that you have a say in. Think about video games, for instance, where you fly fake fighter jets. You can do that, sure. Or you could actually join the military and do it for real. There's no comparison between actually doing something and just fantasizing about it, or talking about it, or criticizing the people who are actually doing it.

There's this great Teddy Roosevelt quote, and it's pretty long, but it's exactly what I'm talking about.

It is not the critic who counts; not the man who points out how the strong man stumbles, or where the doer of deeds could have done them better. The credit belongs to the man who is actually in the arena, whose face is marred by dust and sweat and blood; who strives valiantly; who errs, who comes short again and again, because there is no effort without error and shortcoming; but who does actually strive to do the deeds; who knows great enthusiasms, the great devotions; who spends himself in a worthy cause; who at the best knows in the end the triumph of high achievement, and who at the worst, if he fails, at least fails while daring greatly, so that his place shall never be with those cold and timid souls who neither know victory nor defeat.

That's what I'm talking about. That's how I want you to live your life. Get in the arena. Strive valiantly. Pick yourself up after you fall down and try again, over and over.

People come up to me after they hear me speak and say, "I used to be like that. I knew that instinct at one point in my life. I knew what my gut was telling me. I knew I was here to be the best. But I got beat up too many times, and I just forgot. And then after a while, it was just easier not to go that route anymore. And so I settled for what I have now: this job, and this marriage, and this house, and this way of living."

And so that's where we are in the world. I want you to know that you're like those people who come talk to me. I know what's true to your nature, and that is that you're the best. I'm going to speak to you that way and expect you to surrender to your birthright of being the best. To do this you must behave as if you're the best. Most of the world, including most of the popular culture, is going to speak to you as if you're not the best, as if you're a fan and not a player. But I'm talking to you as you actually are. Does that cause you pain? Are you feeling resistance? If you're telling yourself, *Oh, damn, this is going to be hard,* well, you're in the right place. It is going to be hard. And you'll never regret it.

Shakespeare's play *Henry V* tells about the Battle of

Agincourt, where the English were vastly outnumbered by the French; by some historical estimates, the French had more than twenty thousand warriors and the English had just six thousand. Whatever the exact numbers were, the English were at a huge disadvantage. They weren't ready to fight. They were tired. They were hungry. They were cold. They were sick. And so all King Henry's senior men came to him and said, "We need to wait for more troops to get here, because otherwise we are going to get slaughtered. We need to rest, to eat, to get ready for this battle."

And you know what King Henry said to them? He said, "All things are ready if our minds be so."

All things are ready if our minds be so. That's what I want you to take away from this chapter. That's what separates the player from the fan. Make your mind ready and the rest of your life will follow.

ACTION STEPS

We have several for this chapter. Don't rush through these. They have the power to change your life.

1. List your distractions.

Take a nice deep breath, think about your life, and start writing. I want you to be brutally honest here. Which of your activities are a distraction from actually living? Watching hours of random TV shows? Vacantly scrolling through your social media feeds? Eating mind-lessly? Drinking? Hanging out with people you don't really want to be with? Shopping for and buying stuff you don't need?

Write it all down. Don't be embarrassed; you're the only one who will see this list. It's important to be completely open with yourself about how you distract yourself from living out of your declaration.

2. Circle those you can get rid of in a month.
3. Circle those you can get rid of in a year.
4. Make your "Never Do Again" list.

This step is just what it sounds like. Take a look at your distractions list and decide which of those activities keep you from fulfilling on your promise. The important thing about this list is that it's not going to happen all at once, but you have to write down everything that you're willing to leave behind. Keep that list in a handy place, because you're going to refer to it over the course of the next twenty years. New distractions will come up, and you'll add them to your list. Old distractions will drop off because you've stopped doing them. This list works, but like everything else I'm teaching you, it's a long-term commitment.

To truly make your distractions a thing of the past, fill out your Preparation Exercise at boeason.com/actionsteps. You'll also find what's next with your "Never Do Again" list.

5.

ACCELERATION

*If you don't create and control your environment, your
environment will create and control you.*
—Benjamin Hardy, *Willpower Doesn't Work*

Take a minute to let the quote above sink in. It's one of the most brutally honest things I've ever run across. It also fits in perfectly with this chapter's theme, which is the vital role your environment plays in accelerating and supporting the enormous changes you're making.

This idea of environment is central to your success. You'll run out of steam while attempting to fulfill your dreams if your environment is working against you. And for so many of us, that's exactly what's happening. Hardy writes, "The environment around us is far too powerful, stimulating, addicting, and stressful to overcome by just white-knuckling our way through each day. The only long-term way to stop just surviving and learn how to truly thrive in today's world is to create and control your environment. Lasting personal change, high performance, creativity, and productivity can occur only by strategically outsourcing your desired behavior to goal-enriching environments."

In your life, that means you must take your declaration and find whatever opposes it or will get in its way, then remove those things. Create and control your environment, as Hardy says. So for example, let's say you want to lose fifteen pounds. Or fifty pounds. The number doesn't matter; the approach matters. You have to eliminate all the junk food in your cupboards and in your fridge. You also have to build an environment that surrounds you with people who eat healthy and train regularly. If you can't put yourself in that sort of environment, you'll almost certainly struggle to lose the weight, because the pull of environment is so strong.

Think about how much energy and willpower you use day in and day out just dealing with the environment you're in. So much stuff is constantly coming at us: news, so-called entertainment, video games, Facebook, toxic people. You have to fortify yourself against it as best you can. That usually involves drastically changing your environment.

Your environment must be set up to support your acceleration toward your declaration. Most people think that acceleration means to accelerate past people, to pass them by. So when you watch Usain Bolt, if he's sprinting toward another gold medal in the Olympics, it appears that he's accelerating past other runners to win the race. But the opposite is actually true. What's happening is that he's decelerating at a slower pace than the rest of the field.

It sounds crazy, I know. But it's true. And that's what this chapter is about. I want you to understand that while it looks as if you're passing people by, what's really happening is that they are decelerating faster than you are, so you're going right past them. They're falling back, and you're pulling ahead. That's the key to sustained speed: If you're going to win a race of any length, you must have the ability to decelerate at a slower pace. For us, that means the race lasts ten, fifteen, twenty years, and you have to decelerate at a slower pace than everyone else for those years.

So go back and look at your declaration. Imagine yourself twenty years into the future. And now answer this question: Do you have the stamina to fulfill this twenty-year plan? Can you decelerate at a slower pace than everyone else? Yes? No? Answer it truthfully. And if the answer is yes, that's great. However, if your answer is no, then you have to design a life that will support you fulfilling your declaration. You have to design a life that will move you along the path of your twenty-year plan. That's why I'm placing so much emphasis on environment.

Most of you will answer no. You don't think you have the stamina to pursue this plan for twenty years. There's no shame there; you're being totally honest, which is what I demand from the people I work with. Answer this question: What's going to take you out? What's the one thing that's going to take you out from fulfilling on your destiny? What's the biggest challenge impacting your stamina?

People usually know the exact answer to this question. One man at a recent seminar raised his hand and said, "Alcohol." Another guy said, "Women." Some people are concerned that their energy level wouldn't last that long. Another person said, "My willpower will run out." And they're all right. Everyone is right about what's going to take them out, because they have an instinctive feeling for what their deepest vulnerability is. You probably know exactly what's standing in your way.

This is a really extreme example, but one of my clients decided her family was going to take her out. She said that the biggest sacrifice she ever made was letting her family go, letting go of these people that she genuinely loves, and not being able to take them with her wherever she was going. She said, "They can't call me; they can't text me; they're not allowed in my home. I have to do that because I have to protect my potential. I have to protect what I know I'm capable of. I have to protect that environment. So it's been a huge sacrifice to cut off my family and friends. To say to them, 'You just can't be here.' That was really painful. But in the end, I think it's worth it. You have to create boundaries and protect yourself. You have to play the long game."

It's difficult to have the will to delay gratification, to play the long game, instead of living a life that will ultimately give you regret and pain. But stay the course. Boredom and monotony are going to be the new cool! It's classic to stay the course. Play that game and play it out until you fulfill your declaration.

That's where designing your environment comes in. This needs to happen in all areas of your life. If you want to be focused at work, you need to remove all the distractions from your physical and digital workspace. If you want more creative insights, get out of your town and relax somewhere different for a day or two. If you want to be more motivated, take on greater responsibility and increase the stakes for both success and failure—that will kick up your motivation level.

Remember, your environment is more than just your physical surroundings; it's the people you choose to form relationships with, the information you let in, the foods you consume, the music you listen to, the movies you see—everything external shapes your internal experience.

Put simply, your worldviews, beliefs, and values didn't come from within you. They came from outside of you.

You recall from chapter 4 where I told you that sometimes parents will ask me what's the first thing they should do to support their kid who wants to be a professional athlete, and I tell them, "Turn off sports television." That is a simple but powerful example of building an environment that supports you—or in this case, your child. You have to guard and fortify your life against an environment you don't want your kid to be around.

Sports television isn't inherently bad, but it's for fans, not players. The environment sports television builds is "Athletes are gods, and they're great and they're super-talented, and you are not any of those things. You're good enough to sit on the sidelines and be entertained. Here, have some chips and a beer." And that's why athletes don't watch it. Even though it's made about athletes, it's not made for them.

If you don't shape your environment, it will shape you. If your kid gets a big dose of sports television on a regular basis, he or she will grow up to be a fan of athletes instead of growing up to be an athlete.

Think, for instance, about Lauren Holiday. She didn't grow up watching women play soccer on television. Lauren grew up tagging along after her older brother, playing tackle football with him and his friends, and joining a soccer team because he played soccer. Her home environment shaped and supported her. As an adult, you can shape your home environment to support you; as a parent, you can do this for your kids.

My parents did an amazing job of creating a supportive environment for us. They separated us from people who didn't believe in dreams and people who were naysayers. They just wouldn't let us be around them, and they decided not to be around them, either. My parents were so protective of our dreams that toxic people, toxic points of view, amateurish ways of thinking, victimhood think and talk—none of that was allowed around us. I had friends who I played sports with, and their moms were my mom's friends. These moms would come over and visit, and eventually they'd tell my mom, "Well, we hear your boys have these dreams of playing pro football. You know that no one from around here has ever played pro football, don't you? Aren't they putting all their eggs in one basket? You know their hearts are going to be broken when it doesn't work out, Marilyn." And my mom would literally physically take these people to the front door and eliminate them from our home. So a lot of her friends went away because she and my dad believed in us, and they created an environment that supported our dreams. They expected a lot of us, yes, but they made it possible for us to realize our dreams. And anyone who didn't believe was shown the door.

My brother, Tony, and I would throw and catch the ball so many times per day that if the ball was hitting the ground, it wouldn't last until the following Christmas, when we'd get a new ball. And we sure weren't getting a new ball *before* Christmas. So we figured out a way to get that thing to last by not letting it touch the ground. That became a rule. And I carried that rule over into the home that Dawn and I have created. It's not just about not letting the ball touch the ground; it's about having really high standards for our kids, not coddling them, not expecting less than the best they can deliver.

Axel's twelve now, and we can go outside for two and a half hours and throw the ball around, and it never touches the ground during that whole time. That's the standard we hold to. That's the environment we built. And that's possible not because Axel is gifted or talented in any way. It's because he's already spent thousands of hours throwing and catching a ball, and he's not even a teenager yet.

So build your environment. Stay away from people who don't think it's okay to be great, people who let their kids play video games for hours and hours, people who don't work out, people who aren't committed to their relationships and are cheating on their spouse. You are your environment. Make that choice, day after day, to have your environment support you instead of fight against you.

The environment takes precedence in making your declaration come to life. Because you can have these big dreams for twenty years, but what happens is you run out of steam. We run out of energy before we can live up to that twenty years—we get close to the finish line and *bam,* we're dead or we're hurt or we're incapacitated. So if I want to fulfill my new declaration when I'm seventy-eight or eighty years old, I have to remember the importance of my environment. I have to know how to build the environment that will support me, how to eliminate the things I don't need.

Your environment can change literally everything about your life and your performance. The first day I played pro football, the very first day, I was twenty-one years old, I'd just gotten drafted, and I'd flown straight from UC Davis to Tampa Bay, where Houston was playing. I hadn't gone to training camp, so I hadn't practiced with the team and didn't know any of the players. I had some of their bubblegum cards, yeah, but I'd never met anyone in person.

So I met them in Tampa, went straight into the locker room, put on my stuff, and headed out onto the field. And all of a sudden, I realized just how wild this was. I had played in a Division II college program, right? But here I was, my first play, and I thought, *I'm in the NFL! Damn, look at these guys!* So the ball got snapped, and I started to backpedal, and dudes were running in front of my eyes; I'd never seen people move that fast. James Owens was one of them; he was a wide receiver and an Olympic gold medalist. Anyway, he ran a post pattern right in front of my nose. He blasted right past me. And I thought, *I'm out of here. They're going to get rid of me. Everything's moving way too fast.*

So that was the first down. On the second down, I told myself, *Screw that. They ain't sending me home. I'm staying.* And out of survival, out of primitive instinct, I just turned it up. In one moment, I was this speed, and the very next second, I was a lot faster, because no way was I going to let them send me home. So all of a sudden, my body went as fast as theirs did. And I thought, *Wow, what just happened here?*

So the key to life is you have to put yourself in those situations that aren't comfortable, because that is what will make you great. They're no fun at first. And then you learn how to step up to the challenge, and you think, *Damn, I can pretty much do anything. I can push myself beyond what I'm comfortable with, and it doesn't break me. It makes me stronger.*

Now, this is going to be a little hard to hear, but I'm not going to go easy on you, and I'm sure as hell not going to lie to you: If you fully commit to your declaration, people will drop out of your life. As you change your environment, there will be no real importance or benefit to you in keeping some of your friendships going. You'll notice that when you're around people who don't share your commitment to greatness, they're gossiping, having small-minded conversations, complaining, whining about their lives. And people with a twenty-year plan figure out pretty quickly that that's just not what they want to be around anymore. So your friend group will get smaller. You'll surround yourself with people who have your same mind-set and focus, people with whom you can share the same support system that you are building within your family.

Another thing to keep in mind about shaping your environment is that you can choose to proactively place yourself into situations that demand ten times, a hundred times more from you than you've ever dealt with before. If you do that, you will adapt quickly to that new environment. Crafting highly demanding situations and then mindfully adapting to those situations is the key to success.

This is something Dawn and I do with our clients. They always say to us, "Thank you for building this space for us. Thank you for the safety you provide in this room for us to risk it all and do this deep work."

If you could see my dining room, you'd see these three dream boards that are right there, one for each kid. They've got pictures and dreams of what they want to be. So even though we live in this beautiful, well-designed house, these dream boards and colorful pictures are right there in the open, and they make it clear that this home is an environment of high standards. It's an environment of dreams. And those dreams are on display. They're everywhere. They speak to what we value. We bring our clients into our home environment, because we want them to see how they could create it for themselves if they want to be the best. We have great food, great drinks, great stories, great visiting with people who hold themselves to the same high standards—that's all part of what we model. Everything we do in this home is about nurturing the people who are here, whether they live here or they're visiting.

So you can either create this positive environment and support yourself and your dreams, or you can just do what the majority of the global population is doing and sink into that negative environment, the one that doesn't challenge you to be great. You'll adapt to whatever environment you choose.

Too many of us surround ourselves with people who have mediocre mind-sets, or people who don't want to get healthier, or people who eat crappy food, or people who complain and play the victim. And over time, you get comfortable in that situation and you settle into an environment of mediocrity.

That environment of mediocrity will drive your life outcome if you let it.

Or you could put yourself into a totally different environment, one that supports your declaration, one that demands a lot from you, and see how that influences and improves your life.

Will and Ariel Durant wrote an eleven-volume masterpiece titled *The Story of Civilization*, and I strongly recommend you read it. They made a study of people through time, and they concluded that history is not shaped by great people but rather by demanding situations.

I'm going to repeat that: History is not shaped by great people but rather by demanding situations.

Most of us think that outstanding people like George Washington and Thomas Jefferson are the reason the United States is a country today. And the Durants argue that no, it's not that the men and women of that time were great; it's that what was heaped upon their shoulders was so demanding. They adapted to that demand, and the people around them rose to that level, as well.

It's the demand that brings out the exceptional qualities in a person. I honestly think that the ability of the average person could be doubled if it were demanded of them. And that's what the people who work with me thrive on. They love to be commanded to perform at their top level.

I just can't stress this enough: Your potential is shaped by what surrounds you. Or as the Durants saw it, you're either rising up or shrinking down from the demands of your situation. Most people are living small not because they lack the inherent talent or drive but because their situation isn't demanding more from them. They haven't placed themselves in a position that requires them to become more than they currently are. They just haven't built the right environment.

You need to take the steps to change that situation. You must build the environment that demands that you fulfill your declaration. Most people are not playing a big enough game, and it starts right in their home. If you demand of yourself to run a marathon in six months, your life is different starting right now. You're going to change your environment and stock your home with food that supports your marathon goal. You're going to plan a workout schedule that supports your marathon goal. You're going to change your social life to support your marathon goal.

Science has proved over and over again that there are no shortcuts. You must spend the time to reach your goal. If you show me your schedule, I can predict your future. Amateurs show up on time. Average people show up on time. Whiners and complainers show up on time.

You? You show up early. You're going to add on pre-work and post-work sessions for everything that is in line with your declaration. You put in the hours, and that translates into expertise gained.

I've already told you that Axel wants to play in the NFL and the NBA. He's not going to do that by being naturally gifted or talented or any of that nonsense. He's going to do that because of the hours of practice he puts in. Before every practice, before every game, before every time he works out with a trainer, he goes through a dynamic workout. He's activated by the time other kids are showing up for practice. So you have the other kids being dropped off for a two-hour practice and the practice starts with warm-ups. Well, Axel's already warmed up and ready to go. It's not even a fair fight because he's already so far ahead.

So project that attitude, that commitment, out twenty years into the future. Think about the hours. Think about the control he's taken over his life. Think about how much greater his potential outcome is because of all this practice he's put in.

I want you to do the same thing. If you have a workout session or a rehearsal or a practice or a presentation or a meeting in preparation for a big customer, get there early. Stay there late. That extra practice, those extra hours, taken over time, over years, give you a huge advantage. And it's not because you're gifted or lucky. It's because you've worked your tail off for it.

Suppose somebody said to you right now, "Hey, I can turn you into the seventh-fastest person in the world in thirty days. You want to work with me?" Well, you're getting the hang of it, so you'd say, "Heck, no, this guy is full of it." But every amateur runner in the world would show up, and they'd be lined up out the door, trying to become the seventh-fastest person in the world in thirty days. Because they don't know any better, and they have a short-term mind-set.

Your mind-set is twenty years. Now, in those twenty years you're going to have a lot of successes; it's not like nothing happens until you hit twenty years. But I think of those in-between successes as being goals, and the end result of that twenty years is your dream, what your declaration is about. On the way to your dream, you can have a goal of winning your age group in a race or publishing a book or taking your company to a certain sales level—but that's not the same as your big dream, which is to be the best.

Forget the Past—Start Now

To riff on an old Chinese proverb: The best time to have adopted this mind-set was twenty years ago. The second-best time is right now. So do it now. You're going to be off course most of the time, and that's okay. Your job is to keep your declaration in mind, shape your environment accordingly, and keep righting the ship when you drift off course. You're going to choose the pain and monotony of discipline, of showing up for yourself, over the pain of disappointment. And you're going to make that choice for the next twenty years.

That's the value of a twenty-year plan. That's why shaping and choosing your environment is so vital to fulfilling your declaration. Your environment will shape the person you become and the destiny you have.

According to Ben Hardy, "Environmental design is your greatest responsibility." If you don't pay attention to and shape your environment, you won't reach the top in twenty years, because you'll run out of steam.

I'm telling you this from my viewpoint at a certain age. I'm fifty-eight, and it's only been in the last eight or so years that I've really understood all of this. I've got this wisdom because of all the things I've attempted and all the changes I've gone through. And now, is my body about to run out of gas or could I have a heart attack and never pass on all this wisdom? No way. I'm not letting that happen. I want to fulfill on this. In twenty years, I want to have a relationship with the seventy-eight-year-old me. I want to have a relationship with Dawn. I want relationships with our kids. So what environment do I have to build right now to get there and be the best in the world at what I'm doing when I'm seventy-eight? Well, for sure I have to build an environment of good health, of energy, of vitality. That means I have to eat a certain way. I have to train a certain way. I have to build an environment with as few distractions as possible.

You're probably tired of me talking about eliminating distractions. But if you took one day, or even one half of one day, and jotted down how many times you were interrupted by something, you'd be shocked at how many times it happens. So many people are just running around and distracted all day, every day. They get to the end of a twenty-year cycle and then wonder why they're so exhausted but nothing has really changed. They haven't reached any higher levels or attained any goals. They're completely distracted every time they turn around—they're putting out a fire or dealing with an unexpected text or handling an emergency PTA meeting. A million things will get in your way if you let them. Instead of being loyal to the one thing you should be loyal to, which is your dream, your declaration, you're letting distractions invade your environment. You've read far enough in this book to know that's not how this works. That's not how you bring your declaration to life. You have to eliminate everything that doesn't line up with your declaration. That means junk food, unhealthy people, media distractions, everything, every last little thing that doesn't line up with your declaration has got to go. And when you find things creeping back in—because you will, until you practice this enough that it becomes second nature—you eliminate them again.

It sounds difficult, and it sounds harsh, and at first it will be challenging. But stick with it and I can promise you your life will change for the better. The more things you eliminate, the more streamlined your life will get, and the easier it will be to concentrate on your declaration. If you decide to eliminate a certain type of people, you'll find that they just drop off without you even having to work at it after a while. You'll watch less TV. You'll not be on your phone or computer as much. You won't be attending parties that aren't in line with what you believe.

Basically, you will have fewer and fewer options. It's

just like training for a marathon. In the beginning, you had all these options. Then you made a declaration, a commitment, that you're going to run this long, arduous race. So now a lot of your options disappear. The option of drinking two beers every night goes away. The option of eating a bad breakfast before your ten-mile run goes away. The option of reading text messages or checking Facebook while you train goes away.

It sounds magical, but it's true. Things go away from you when you make this kind of declaration. That's why I demand that my clients make the declaration to be the best at their thing, because only then will we know what they've got. That's why I'm demanding the same from you.

You've got your list of distractions that you made at the end of the last chapter. Look it over again. Sit quietly with those distractions for a few minutes, and you'll understand on a gut level that you can have those distractions, that drama, that gossip, that junk food. Or you can be the best in the world. And every day, minute to minute, hour to hour, you have to decide. You have to course-correct constantly. And you just do it, because otherwise you won't realize your dream. How you feel right now—whatever temptation you're feeling right now, whether it's to eat some junk food or skip a workout or sleep in late or show up just barely on time—if you put that up against your twenty-year plan, your plan is going to win. Your declaration takes precedence over how you're feeling. And when you mess up, you get back to your declaration. Because otherwise, I can guarantee you that in twenty years, you will look back at this time and you will be overwhelmed with regret.

As you make those decisions, keep in mind that the very word *decide* is about eliminating things. The root of the word *decide, cide,* is from a Latin word that means killing off or cutting off everything else. Isn't that amazing? Your course of action is right there in this ancient word. Once you decide, you've closed off the other options. Suicide, homicide, genocide, decide—you're killing something. But in the case of *decide,* you get to turn away from all those options you've killed off and bring your declaration to life.

These next two action steps will help you bring your decision, your declaration, to full and vibrant life.

ACTION STEPS

1. Get the distractions list that you made at the end of chapter 4. Now, divide that list into three sections: distractions you can get rid of tomorrow, distractions you can get rid of in a month, and distractions you can get rid of in a year. Keep that list with you. Make a copy and put it up in your bathroom or on your bedside table or somewhere you'll see it every day. Eliminate, eliminate, eliminate.

2. Now that it's really clear what your distractions are, design your environment. If you're going to

lose weight, go through your house and get rid of the junk food. Don't leave yourself any junk food options in the house. Go to the store and bring home healthy food that will support your declaration. Or if you've listed social media as one of your distractions, delete the apps from your phone or your computer. Facebook or Instagram or Twitter or Pinterest or wherever you mindlessly waste time—be brutal. Delete it. If it's distracting you, it has to go. Otherwise, in twenty years, you'll be looking back thinking, *Crap, I wasted thousands of hours looking at other people's lives and didn't bother to live my own life.* If the sort of people you're hanging out with are your distraction, make a vow that you'll change your social life. Are you hanging out with people who are positive and focused on being great and uplifting the people around them? Or are you surrounded by whiners and gossipers who drink too much, tear other people down, and eat junk? You're the only one who can make this change, and it might hurt. But I can guarantee you that your declaration is unattainable if the people in your environment aren't up to your standards.

6.

DOMINATION

Domination. Here's another word, like *competition*, that has really taken a beating lately. We're told we're not supposed to dominate the people around us and that we can't dominate without doing harm to others. We need to be nice and kind and gentle. Domination is bad. Cooperation is good.

Well, here's what I think of when I use the word *domination:* You have to dominate yourself, not so much the people around you. You have to surrender your full loyalty and commit to what your spirit is calling out of you. What's getting in the way of what you're called to be in this life? Dominate those things that you are allowing to block you from fulfilling your declaration.

That's domination.

Shannon Crownover: Dominating Your Mind-Set

Shannon is one of my Mastermind and Personal Story Power attendees, and I've seen enormous progress over the years. Her story has a lot to do with dominating your mind-set:

When I first saw Bo onstage, I didn't really like him because he was tapping into something deep inside of me that I was scared to reveal. There was no way in hell I was going to get up onstage and share my personal story like he did! I figured if that's what it took for me to be the best, for me to have the impact I wanted to have on women, it wasn't worth it.

But at the end of the first day, something he said really hit home: "You don't have to be the best. You can go home and just sit there and continue to do what you've always done. Just stay in your comfort zone. That's what most people do. They give up on their dreams. Or you can be one of the few who actually try to make this world a better place." With those words, Bo totally shifted my worldview of what it takes to be the best. He has this way of scaring you but also showing you that it's possible to be the best and that you can learn how to do it.

The Mastermind program was way more money than I thought I could afford, but making that commitment helped me know that I would show up and do it. Bo pushed me hard. After I gave my three-minute story the

first time, he said, "Shannon, what are you holding back?"
I told him I didn't like my story or believe it was anything
special. And then I got tears in my eyes. And he said,
"That's what we want. I like this Shannon, with the emotion showing! We want the real you. We want the vulnerable you, putting yourself on the line for us, not some
robot up there who's just delivering the words of her
story." So I had to go through this journey of getting it all
out, working through all that emotion and giving myself
credit for the huge things I'd done, like being a single
working mom living far from family and raising my two
girls—all these little daily battles that I'd fought and won
that I'd just tossed aside like they were nothing special.
And in that process, I was able to find my own love for
myself and for my own story. It was the first time I'd ever
realized, *Oh my God, that was hard as hell, and I did it
and I did it well.*

Eventually, I brought that get out-of-your-comfort-
zone attitude to my full-time job at the Nature Conser-
vancy. We've been around for sixty years, and in the past
two years, we've gone through a huge mission evolution.
We're not just about protecting nature for nature's sake;
now we're about protecting nature for people's sake and
for nature's sake. I shifted my own role at work by speaking up using my voice, which I didn't really do before I
met Bo. I told the organization's leaders that we all need
a personal story and to bring more emotion to our work.
To be the best organization, we need to be the best

leaders, and that means putting our hearts on the line. We have to talk about our core values as an organization, not just our strategy or science, and connect with people more quickly in a more personal way.

Finally, working with Bo has transformed my marriage. I had always thought that being feminine meant being weak and overly emotional. But I learned through observing Bo and Dawn's relationship that authentic femininity has real strength. Now I'm putting everything I've learned from Bo to work in simplifylove.com, the company I launched with my husband, Ricardo. It's a full-time endeavor for him and part-time for me. At first, Ricardo focused on personal development, and I focused on women's confidence coaching, but Bo encouraged us to work together as a couple and to focus on helping other couples. That was a huge breakthrough for us. We launched our first online program in early 2018. Thanks to our work with Bo, we have such a strong foundation that we just keep accomplishing our goals and setting new ones.

When I start to have the inevitable doubts about the dreams Ricardo and I have, or if I'm questioning how to handle an obstacle or sticky situation, I just repeat my dream and ask myself, *What would someone who is the best lover in the world do?* (Meaning loving my entire world of friends, community, family, and of course, Ricardo.) By reminding myself to be this person now in the present, I am constantly achieving in little ways the big dream every day.

Prepare, Perform, Recover

One way to get started on this domination is to get clear about what you should be doing every day. I'm not talking about a long list of daily tasks. You need just three things. You need to be preparing to perform, performing, or recovering from performing. If you're not doing one of those three things, you know your business is losing money.

That sounds crazy, but I'm serious. Just name three things that you do that fit those three things in your world. These are three things that are making your business or your dream grow, and you know that when you're doing one of those three things, the business or dream is coming into existence. If you're not doing one of those three things, you know either you're going out of business or your dream is dying.

Remember we talked about course correction? You know when you're off base. It's really clear to you, if you're honest, that either you're building the dream or you're tearing the dream down. Either you're fulfilling your declaration or you're tearing your declaration apart. Either you're on course or you're in need of course correction. But you're never in the middle, you're never complacent, you're never just staying the same.

You're either building or you're not building. It's that simple.

I love that concept, and I want you to take it to heart. You'll hear people say, or you might say, "Well, I think I'm just going to hang today and take it easy." And my response to that is always, "Sure, go ahead. But your dream is going out of business while you're just hanging around."

Figure out what your three things are and make sure you're doing them. This is something that all the best competitors and performers do. Think about some of the top performers in the world, both past and present—Tom Brady, Simone Biles, Serena Williams, Mikhail Baryshnikov, Frank Sinatra. They're doing one of three things, and that's how they got to the heights they did. Either they're preparing to perform, or they're performing, or they're recovering from performing. Doesn't matter what their discipline or art form is, that's their pattern to reach the top and stay there.

And that's what my life is. Anything I'm doing that is not one of those three things, I know my business is now going downward. So if I'm folding laundry, and that's not recovery for me, and that's not preparation for me, then I'm going south on my business, because folding laundry is not performance for me! If I'm recovering, I might be resting, sleeping, getting a massage, working on my presentation, or other things like that. I know my business is building, because I'm taking care of myself so that I can get back onstage and train people to be the best at what they do.

I can't overstate how important this is. You actually are calling the shots. You can say, "I'm not going to build my business today. I'm going to do chores, or I'm going to grocery shop, or I'm going to goof off." If doing chores is part of your recovery, then that's fine. I like to wash the dishes, for instance. Sometimes I practice my talks while I'm washing dishes, and Eloise, my daughter, will say, "What did you say, Dad?" and I'll just say, "Oh, nothing, honey, just practicing." I know that for some people, cooking is part of their recovery, or working around the house. My point is you're the one who knows where things fit or don't fit in your life and whether or not those things are part of the three things you need to do every day. For a lot of people, recovery can include having a nap or resting after you perform. The performance is stressful, but it's positive stress, and then you need to have some sort of proactive rest or recovery afterward.

And if you don't get that recovery and rest period, you're going to run out of steam. You won't be able to perform very long or very well.

I see this most often with people who are trying to handle everything on their own. Well, guess what? You can't handle everything by yourself. You cannot do this on your own.

People I work with hate hearing this. If you're like most of them, especially the really high-achieving women, you're used to doing almost everything on your own. Career, kids, home, bills, community, everything else. You're doing it on your own. You're thinking you can shop, you can cook, you can recover, you can do whatever you do and be the best in the world at it. And I'm telling you that, sorry, you just can't.

A beautiful example of this is from the founder of Strategic Coach, Dan Sullivan. He talks about how Frank Sinatra didn't move pianos. And your first reaction is "What the hell? Of course Frank Sinatra didn't move pianos. He sang." But think about it. What did Frank Sinatra actually do? He walked onstage and he sang. And before that, he was warming up and getting ready to sing. After he sang, he recovered from singing so that he could move into the preparation cycle again. He didn't sell tickets. He didn't usher people into the auditorium and seat them. He didn't promote himself. He didn't sell refreshments in the lobby. He didn't book venues for his concerts. He didn't do all that stuff that had to happen for a Frank Sinatra concert to work. He just did what he did, which was to sing.

Frank Sinatra was able to do that because he had a team.

The Team Behind the Person

The next time you go to a concert or a sporting event or a play—anything at all, really, that involves someone performing—I want you to look beyond the performers. Don't just see them. See the team behind them.

Take Tom Brady, for instance. He might be the best quarterback ever. The next time you watch him play, I want you to think about who's behind the scenes for him. Who makes it possible for him to perform the way he does? Because I can guarantee you that Tom Brady does three things: He trains, he plays, and he recovers. He has people telling him what to eat and when to eat it. He has massage therapists, weight trainers, people who keep his body in top shape.

He's got a team behind him, and I don't mean the other New England Patriots players.

Recently, I thought back on the two prior occupations I had, which were playing in the NFL and being a Broadway playwright and performer. When I was in the NFL, I played the game, and that was my job. If I wasn't playing, I was preparing to play or I was recovering from playing.

So who were the people who made it possible for me to play? Well, let's see. A chiropractor, a massage therapist, a nutritionist, an agent, a financial adviser, a trainer, a doctor, the guys taping my ankles, the equipment managers. That's before you even get to the coaches. You've also got the people who sell tickets to the game, and sell hot dogs at the game, and run the parking garages, and broadcast the games on TV and radio, and write newspaper articles about the games.

So I got to do what I did because there was this whole team behind me doing what they did.

Then I went into a completely different occupation. After I wrote the play and got a stage for it, my job was to perform the play. If I wasn't performing, I was preparing to perform. And if I wasn't doing that, I was recovering from performing.

I'll always remember when we opened in New York City with the one-man play I'd written. It had been just me and Dawn up until that point; Dawn was my fund-raiser and producer; I was the performer. So we finally got this deal in New York with producers and a director and a theater. We made it, right?

I had been walking into theaters for years by this point, just me and Dawn, theaters all over the country. And now I walk into this theater and there are like fifty guys on the stage building the set. And the lighting crew is over on another part of the stage, and the director and his assistant are waiting for us. The money guy is there, the stagehands, the makeup person, my movement coach, my voice coach, my acting coach, my publicist.

It was a one-person show—one person who wrote something—and now that something employed about a hundred people. And that's what I mean when I say I want you to make it a habit to see the team behind the person. Because there's no way I could have accomplished what I did on my own. From the start, I had my parents behind me, and then I had football professionals behind me, then I had Dawn, then I had a whole crew for the play, and now I have another crew that gets me onstage to speak to huge crowds or sends me into smaller places to work with an elite group of highly focused people. My crew handles everything behind the scenes. Everything.

I'm not saying you need a big crew. You absolutely don't, especially not at first. To be the best at what you do, you're going to start with one person on your team, and then you're going to surround yourself with a small Delta Force of elite experts who will help you get where you're going. You need a focused team that takes stuff away. Being the best at what you do is about cutting out, eliminating, and streamlining, remember? You've got to take that seriously. You've got to have a partner who does that for you, and then a team who help your partner do that.

Natural Leadership

Worried about building a team? Maybe you think you're not a leader? Don't be. It will happen automatically.

Lauren Holiday says, "I was never the normal *yell, scream, 'hey, guys, look at me, follow me'* sort of leader. I've built my leadership by building relationships and building trust. When people can trust you, and they know that you're going to give all that you've got every single game and that you've always got the team's best interests in mind and not your own, that builds trust. And when you have the trust of your teammates, you're a leader. I took so much pride in that trust and in being consistent, showing people every day who I am, and not wavering from that. I feel strongly about things, and I don't change my mind easily. My experience is that when people see your own commitment, they will follow you as a leader."

All you need to do is follow your dream with unrelenting passion. The rest will follow.

Finding Your Team

You need someone who is unwavering in the fight for your creativity so that you can risk it all, knowing you have a soft landing. They're willing to deal with no money coming in. They're willing to deal with the body bags. They're willing to deal with no success. They'll fight and fight and fight. And guess what you get at the end of that? A true partnership.

You can't do this alone. I know that's hard to hear, especially if you're a woman and you've been handling things alone—everything from your career to your kids to everything else in your life. You need to step back and let someone help you.

I say to the people I work with, "You're a performer, and you're great at it. You know how to perform, but you really suck at marketing, you suck at keeping your bills paid, you can't even pick out your own clothes for when you're presenting on a stage. You need someone to manage you. You need a Dawn." I can say this to them, because that's what I'm like. It's not an insult. It's just a statement of fact.

And people might resist it at first, but then they'll come back to me and say, "Bo, I found my Dawn. His name is George."

Trust me on this. You need a Dawn.

My wife, Dawn, has been clearing forests for me since 1998 so that I can be my best. Years ago, right before we got married, we were unemployed actors. And one day, I said to her, "Sweetie, I'm going to tell my story, and I'm going to write a play."

Can you imagine? We were about to get married. I'd never written a play. I'd never written anything. I couldn't spell. But I told her I had to write this play because I had to express myself somehow or else I was going to run someone over. We didn't have kids at the time, but I had this vision of us with three kids, and we were pushing a shopping cart down Sunset Boulevard. I thought that was where we were going to end up. I didn't know. But I knew I had to write this play.

I asked her, "Are you cool with that?"

"Yeah," she said. "I'm cool with that."

From that moment on, she's always given me the space to fall on my face, to risk it all, all the time.

When the play was finally done and we were taking it around the country, we would say to each other, "It's just you and me, baby." We would be backstage in theaters, and it was just us. There was nobody else really believing in this thing or what we were going to do. We'd have a packed house of a couple of hundred people out in the audience, and it was just us, alone, backstage, getting ready for another show, never knowing if there was going to be a next show after this one. There was nothing. We just fought for it. And we made it happen.

Now, understand that your commitments will sometimes be offensive to people. That is going to happen. People will say, "Well, you're too big for your britches. Who are you to be the best?" I always go back to Mother Nature, because she is undefeated. She never loses. So I just do what she does. I keep trying and trying, and eventually, I win. When you practice outside your comfort zone, the zone changes you.

If you're truly committed to greatness, you just have to face facts. There's one way to get there, and it's sobering. It is exhausting. It's not like the cover of *People*. It never looks like that. It looks like shit. *You* look like shit, and you're all hunched over like after a brutal run, and you've got slobber coming out of your mouth. That's what being the best looks like. It's alone, cold, damp. It's feeling "Screw this" a lot of the time. But stay the course. One day, all those people in your life who said it was too hard, why would anyone want to do that, that's too cocky, or that's conceited—one day those people will pay money to come watch you perform, or to buy your books, or to take your seminars, or to do business with you instead of someone less committed.

For you to fulfill your declaration and to be the best at what you do, there's no thinking, no options, and no timelines. I love great food, but going shopping for it is not a good use of my time. I love to train physically, but thinking about what I'm going to do at the gym is not a good use of my time. There are some things I just can't think about anymore. All I want to do is do what I do best.

My brother and I attended a basketball camp when we were kids. We were so excited to be there. We wanted to be good basketball players. We wanted to impress the coaches. We wanted to see how we measured up against these other basketball players. So on the first day of practice, we were out there on the gymnasium floor, and there were probably 100 or 150 other attendees. The coach came out, and the first thing he said was, "Okay, campers, here's the deal. Right now, we're going to separate the thoroughbred racehorses from the donkeys."

I remember freezing in my Converse high-tops when he said *donkeys*. I did not want to be a donkey. I looked up at my brother, and he was looking down at me. We silently communicated, *I want to be a racehorse. I want to win.* We worked our tails off until we became those racehorses.

Later, I learned this about thoroughbreds. The thing that separates a thoroughbred from every other horse is a singular ability. They can do the same thing over and over and over again without losing enthusiasm. Other horses work hard, but they get distracted and bored. They can't do it. They're not thoroughbreds.

You can turn yourself into a racehorse. You just have to commit to your declaration and practice over and over and over again until you master it.

If you really want to dominate, you have to figure out where in your life you're making the most impact. If you make the most impact by speaking onstage, your team's job is to get you onstage. You're just the racehorse that goes straight into the gates. In your business, with your family, in your community, you've got to think about where you are a thoroughbred. I bet you're doing a ton of things right now that are making you a donkey.

From this day forward, you are a racehorse. You do one thing. You run fast. And your team will show up and support you in your race.

Once your team gets assembled, let them run with it. Let your Dawn, for instance, tell you what to do. Everyone thinks it's so clever to be the big thinker and the big-idea person. Not me. I don't want to think about anything. I want to do what I do. I want to be on a stage talking to people or be in little groups talking with people. I don't want to worry about how many reps I'm going to do at the gym or how much weight I'm going to lift. I don't want to think about what I'm going to eat. I don't want to think about what stage I'm getting on next or how I'm getting there or what hotel I'm going to stay in. That's not what I do. What I do is I train people to be the best at what they do. And I can't do that if my brain is trying to handle all the behind-the-scenes stuff. That's not what I'm good at.

Keep in mind, it's taken me some years to assemble this team of mine. And I am completely dedicated to my team. Your team will be depending on you to take the lead, so don't expect a team to show up if you're not showing up for yourself. That's not how this works. You have to take the first steps. You have to make your declaration. You have to work your ass off. You have to show that you are fully committed. You have to work harder than anyone else.

You do that, and your team will show up for you.

A Dawn Named Jrue

As you've seen, Lauren Holiday used many of the same principles I'm writing about here. Even to the point of finding her own Dawn—in her case, his name is Jrue:

Jrue and I met and became friends when I was a senior and he was a freshman. He left after his freshman year to play in the NBA, and we kept in touch kind of loosely. My draft was in Philadelphia, which is where he played at the time. We reconnected while I was there, but I didn't want to date. I was extremely focused on playing soccer and starting in a World Cup game. I wanted to be the best I could be in my sport, and I felt like I wouldn't have any time for a relationship.

I told him, and he said, "Well, I'll be there when you have time. What can I do? How can I help? How can I be with you while you go through this?" We stayed in touch and eventually became a couple, which isn't easy for two professional athletes. His schedule was insane, my schedule was insane, but we pushed each other and supported each other as much as we could. I would be with him when I could. He came to the World Cup in 2011, and to the Olympics in 2012, and to the World Cup in 2015.

He's always been such a constant for me. The encouragement, the support, the understanding—I couldn't have asked for a better partner. Every time he watched a game, he always thought that I was the best player. He was a steady voice telling me he thought I was the best. He told me that I could do it, that I could do anything.

When I did finally decide to retire, I looked to Jrue for confirmation. I remember almost begging for his opinion. But he reminded me that it was not his decision, and no matter what that decision was, it needed to be mine and mine alone. He didn't want to have any influence over it. He knew soccer was my passion, and he didn't want to hold me back. That was really cool of him, because he could have said, "Yeah, we see each other three days a month; I want you to retire, I want you to be at home, I want to see you more." But he never, ever said that. He always just said, "When you're ready, that's when you're ready. We'll make it work."

Building Your Team

I tend to trust my gut a lot, and I know, based on the energy of a person, who not to tell my declaration to and who to tell it to. You won't broadcast your declaration all over the place, but you do have to go a little bit public with it. It holds you more accountable if you make a public declaration; once you do, you know that at least one person is waiting for you to deliver on something. That adds positive pressure and accountability.

You'll find that for the most part if you really tune in to the people in your life, you'll be able to tell who you should share your declaration with. Some people will be absolutely on board and will ask how they can help, or tell you they know how to do something that you haven't yet figured out, or offer to put you in touch with someone who has the skills and resources you need.

But of course, there will be people who will tell you you're crazy and there's no way you can make your dream happen. You might have those people in your family. You might have them in your church or your gym or your friend group. Don't flip out when they aren't supportive.

Don't spend your energy trying to get them to believe in you. Just walk away.

Does that sound harsh? You might be worried or feel disloyal about leaving them behind. Here's the thing. You're leaving those people behind, but they are leaving you, too. They're going to stay away from you once you declare that you want to be the best, because it points out their life to them. It exposes too much of their short-comings to be around you. They're going to be think-ing, *Well, darn, I'm not trying to be the best at anything. I'm just getting by. I thought that was good enough. That should be good enough! Who the hell does he think he is?*

And it's good that this happens, that you separate from these sorts of people. Because they're definitely going to be mean. And they're going to point you out. And they're going to mock you. That's just part of the territory when you're blazing this new trail for yourself. So you stay away from them. You don't go to parties and hang out with them. They're not your people anymore.

This dropping away will help you with assembling your team. Your team leader will be able to show up if there's a vacuum where he or she should be. It sounds crazy, but you just need to have faith, be patient, and be-lieve in it, and this person will show up. They will be attracted to the declaration, and they'll want to help you make it happen.

This is one of the reasons your declaration has to be so big. If you make a mediocre declaration, you're going to get a mediocre person showing up to be on your team. But if your declaration is big, if it's impossible, if it's completely over the top, then the right person will show up. In fact, that person might be standing next to you right now with no game to play. You give them something to believe in, and they will show up for you. They need a player to play the game—that's you—so that they can do what they do.

I can't stress enough how important it is to have strong people who believe in you and will help you on your path. My parents did that in so many ways, and not just when we were little kids. My dad went to college at Cal Poly, and he played football there. He was a really good player, captain of the team, a standout. In the middle of his college career, he got drafted to fight in the Korean War. So he went to Korea, fought two years on the front lines, then came back to Cal Poly to play his last two years of college football.

So my dad was loyal to Cal Poly, right? Fast-forward to me and my brother both wanting to play pro football. My dad thought, *Well, maybe my boys will follow in my footsteps and play for Cal Poly. I'm an alum; they know me there; I'll take them there to check it out.*

He arranged for us to go watch Cal Poly play and then meet the head coach in his office the next day. I was probably fifteen years old, my brother was seventeen or so, and our dad really wanted us to go to his college. So we went to the game. Cal Poly got their butts kicked, but we were just excited to be there watching college football and thinking maybe we could play for Cal Poly. The next morning, we went to this meeting in the head coach's office. My dad said to the head coach, "These are my two boys, and they'd like to play football here."

And the guy took one glance at us and said to my brother, "You're too slow; you'll never be able to play quarterback here." And he looked at me and said, "You're too small. You could never play football at this university."

And before he could even finish that sentence, my dad literally put his hands over my ears so I couldn't hear this coach tell me I couldn't play football there, and he lifted me straight up out of my seat with his hands over my ears and threw me out into the hallway, and he did the same thing to my brother. And we immediately went out to my dad's pickup truck and drove the five hours home.

That was a long, uncomfortable drive. No one said a word. We were all so pissed. But I love it that my dad would not even let us listen to that guy tell us we weren't good enough. That's a grizzly bear parent. That's someone who will protect your mentality at all costs. That's the sort of person you need on your team.

Sometimes I think about that coach, and I wonder if he knows Tony was a first-round draft pick for the New England Patriots and I was a second-round pick for the Houston Oilers. I wonder if he knows how wrong he was. And I wonder how many other high school kids he spoke to like that, and if they had anyone guarding their dreams for them.

Re-Compete

"The first biological lesson of history is that life is a competition." Will and Ariel Durant said this in their book *The Lessons of History*. It seems pretty obvious, right? You and I wouldn't be here today if our ancestors didn't win the competition for food, shelter, and mates. But we've moved so far from our own nature that no one wants to compete. In fact, *competition* is now a bad word in our society—kind of like *domination*.

We don't have to learn to compete; competing is a human attribute. But I believe that we have to relearn to compete, or to *re-compete,* as I've dubbed it.

Let me tell you about something I see happening that really bugs me. I call it *stacking the teams and killing the opponents.* If you follow sports at all, you know what I'm talking about: athletes who jump from team to team, sometimes as young as middle school, to play with the best possible team.

"Ah, c'mon, Bo," you're saying. "What's wrong with that? Everybody wants to play on the winning team!"

But there's a fundamental problem with that line of thinking. In real life, playing on the winning team will not necessarily make you a better player. It won't make you a stronger competitor. It will just make you part of a winning team. And if your team wins all the time, you don't have to call on your best skills. You can give less than 100 percent. You don't improve over time because you're not challenged.

I saw this happen on my son's basketball team. He

and a few of his friends wanted to learn how to play basketball, so they formed a team and entered one of Los Angeles's traveling leagues. They were bad. Like, unbelievably bad. They regularly got beaten by thirty, forty points. But they hung in there. They kept practicing. They kept competing. And gradually they improved.

The first time they won a game, they won by a single point over a really good team. Right after the game ended, that team's best player and his parents walked up to our coach and said, "We want to join your team."

So now we had this great player on the team. And the team kept getting better, and more good players kept switching from their teams to my son's team, and now my son's team is the best in the league. They beat other teams by forty points or more almost every game. They don't just win. They crush the other teams. They annihilate them.

You'd think the players would love it, right? Well, they don't. There's no thrill left. There's no competition. There's no risk. They're not becoming better players; instead, they're just going through the motions each game.

It's happening on the pro level, too—teams that are so stacked with outstanding players that other teams just don't stand a chance.

But now there's a cultural shift going on. I'm hearing from college coaches that they don't want the kids who've moved around from high school to high school, chasing the best teams. They want the kids who have stayed loyal, who have gutted it out, who have challenged themselves to play against the players who make them work the hardest and improve their skills. They want the kids who are true competitors.

In anything—sports, novels, movies, life—you need challenge and uncertainty to make things interesting. You need to be forced to bring your best. Without that, you stop changing and growing as a person. You stop improving.

That's not the road to domination. That's the road to elimination, and that's not what your twenty-year plan is about. Your plan is about commitment, about competition, about rising to be the best at what you do. It's about collecting successes along the way, stumbling more times than you can count, and course-correcting constantly.

Let's keep moving toward your dream.

ACTION STEPS

1. Name the three things that you must do every single day to keep your dream or your business building. Write them down and put them up around your house. Remember, if you're not doing one of those three things, your declaration is not moving forward.

2. Start looking for your Dawn. Who can you tell your dream to? Use your gut when you decide who to share your declaration with. Your team will come to you, but remember, you have to make it

happen. And you make it happen by working so hard that your team is attracted to you, starting with your Dawn.

3. The next time you see someone successful, look more closely. See the team behind them. Make a list of all the team members and what you think they do. Now cast your mind a few years into the future. What team members do you think you might need? Do you know anyone who has the skills you need? If not, don't worry. They'll show up for you if you consistently show up for yourself, I promise.

7.

ACCOUNTABILITY

When I was a kid, every so often, my dad would sit down with my brother, Tony, and me and show us his high school and college yearbooks. Tony and I mostly wanted to look at the pictures of the football and basketball teams. And while we looked, Dad would tell us the stories of all his teammates.

"Look at that guy with the huge ears, Dad!"

"Yeah, he was a hell of a player," I remember my dad saying. "That guy really had a chance to be great. But he started drinking, and all of a sudden, he had no chance."

My dad would point out the guys who went off course—alcohol, drugs, partying in general—and didn't recover. They never amounted to much, never accomplished much in their lives. And my brother and I would look at each other and go, "Man, I don't want to be *that* guy. I want to be the guy who goes all the way."

Now, as a dad myself, I think about my dad's genius in telling stories. For me, bad parenting is like, "Hey, boys, let me sit you down and tell you stuff. I don't want you drinking. I don't want you smoking. You can't do that. It's bad for your health." Now, no kid's going to listen to that, right? Especially if after you tell your kid not to drink and smoke, you plop down on the couch with a cigarette and a cold brew. But kids will listen to stories of real people. They'll learn from those stories and really take them to heart. I mean, here it is fifty years later, and I'm remembering the stories of these guys I never knew, all because my dad told us about them.

When I think back on those guys, and I try to figure out why they messed up so badly, I don't think it's just because they got off track and smoked weed and drank. It's because they didn't course-correct. Remember that we're all off course most of the time, just like that jet flying to Maui. It's normal. It's nothing to be ashamed of. The problem comes when we don't course-correct. And most of us don't course-correct because we don't have anyone holding us accountable, and because we're ashamed that we've gotten lost, and because we tell ourselves horrible stories about what it means about us that we've messed up. We don't feel like we deserve a second chance, much less a third or fifth or ninety-ninth chance.

These guys didn't have anyone to tell them, "You messed up. It's okay. You're human. We all mess up. Don't be ashamed of yourself. Just pick yourself up, brush your-self off, and start again."

They didn't have anyone to hold them accountable.

The toughest part of bringing your dream into exis-tence, bringing your declaration into existence, is stay-ing accountable. What I'm going to give you in this chapter is a way to build accountability right into your life.

I use—and I have my clients use—three levels of ac-countability. If you only use one level of accountability, you'll lose your way. You need backups, so that when one way fails (and it will!), you've got two others supporting you and helping you course-correct.

1. You have to build your environment. This means laying down the structure that will keep you ac-countable for the next twenty years. It's like build-ing a house. The foundation comes first.

2. You need partnerships and human relation-ships. You simply can't do this alone. It takes too much energy, and it's no fun.

3. You're going to schedule your championships—your major goals and measurements along the path. Twenty years is a long time. You need a way to measure your progress in smaller increments of time.

Build Your Environment

When you build your environment, your life becomes much easier. Build it correctly, and you save yourself a tremendous amount of energy that you would otherwise have to put into stamina and willpower.

I talked earlier about structuring your environment so that it supports you—for instance, if you're going to lose fifty pounds, go through your kitchen and get rid of all the unhealthy foods, then bring in healthy foods. There's another, more detailed level of environment building, however, and it revolves around time and how to section out your time so that you know exactly what you're doing and when.

Let's assume you've made your declaration and you're looking at a twenty-year window of time to make your declaration come into being. That is a huge block of time. You have to break it down into smaller chunks and use those chunks to propel you toward your goal. It's like building a house—piece by piece, you put the structure in place that will keep you accountable for the next twenty years.

My favorite way of breaking time down into meaningful chunks comes from a study done by Dr. Jane Wardle and Dr. Phillipa Lally of University College London. They found that it takes sixty-six days to acquire a habit (longer than the thirty days we've all heard of), but that once you do something for sixty-six days in a row, it will be harder *not* to do it than to actually do it.

Think about that. It will take less energy to do this

thing you want to do than not to do it. That's essentially hacking into your brain and body and rewiring yourself.

How can you put the study's findings to work? Let's say your declaration is to be the best writer. Obviously, your smaller goals along the way would be to write several books or movie scripts or plays or whatever your type of writing might be. You've got twenty years—how are you going to become the best? You might start with a sixty-six-day commitment to write every single day. Write for an hour, write a thousand words, whatever it is you decide to do. Just commit to doing it for sixty-six days. And on day sixty-seven, you'll find yourself unable to go without writing. It's so ingrained in you at that point that it's easier to just write the darn words than not to write them.

Committing to a short-term goal that's part of your multiyear declaration makes all the difference. If you're looking at a twenty-year window of time, that can seem like a cross-continental trip on a dusty old cattle track. How the hell are you going to get from here to there? The sixty-six-day chunks of time are like widening and paving that cattle track one foot at a time. Every day, every week, every month, you pave another section, and you just keep moving forward.

You know by now that I love using examples from my own family, both the one I grew up in and the one Dawn and I have created. With Axel's dream of playing in the NFL and the NBA, we've had to break down his larger dream into lots of smaller goals. We've done sixty-six-day windows to work on nutrition, to work on his speed, to work on his ball handling. Each window has a theme, so to speak, and when he gets done with one, he goes on to the next.

Eloise, our daughter, has a dream to be the best performer, whether as a pastry chef or as a performer on Broadway. So how do you make that happen? Well, you start by breaking it down to everything you need to be able to do onstage. You'll have to be able to dance, to sing, to act. So you tackle pieces of that declaration one by one. Is it voice class coupled with ballet class for sixty-six days in a row? Is it more specific—are you going to master the plié in the next sixty-six days? How about committing to a voice warm-up every day for sixty-six days? Guess what, after the sixty-six days are over, you can't *not* do your voice warm-up. It's part of you now. It's actually harder to skip it than it is to do it. It takes less energy to do it than not.

Now, if you want to, inside the theme of each sixty-six-day period, you can put what I call a *marker*. Let's say you're working on a novel and your current sixty-six-day goal is to write fifty pages. A marker would be to practice your dialogue skills or your secondary character development skills during those sixty-six days.

You can break it down as much as you want, into whatever pieces you want, as long as they all point toward your long-term goal.

Then when you're at the end of one sixty-six-day chunk of time, you decide on the next one. As you successfully close out one window, your next theme will become obvious to you. I don't plan them out ahead of time. I find that if I concentrate on paving one section of that cross-continental track, the next section becomes apparent. The correct way keeps appearing as I go along.

What you're doing with those smaller windows of time is laying down the structure, the foundation, that your bigger dream is going to grow on. You don't just decide, *Hey, I'm going to be the best writer,* and then wake up the next morning and you're the best writer. No. You work for it. You practice. You take writing workshops or get a writing coach or writing partners. You read everything you can get your hands on. And you keep after it for decades, with smaller goals and tasks along the way to build up your skill as a writer.

So what does all of this have to do with building your environment? Well, you're going to put together a sixty-six-day board that has your current theme on it, because visual reminders are a vital part of your environment. When I was younger, I had pictures of Walter Payton and Mike Reinfeldt in my locker and at home. Every time I opened my locker and saw those pictures, I was reminded of where I was headed. That's what the pictures are for. Even if you're having a bad day, you're tired, you're weak, you ate too much chocolate, you're sick, whatever, you see those pictures, and it trips a wire in your brain. *Okay, right. That's where I'm headed. Time to get back on track.*

I'm a huge believer in what are now called *vision boards,* but with one key difference. As far as I can tell, vision boards are just about cutting out pictures of what you want and letting the universe or someone outside yourself make it all appear like magic. That's not how this works! The vision boards we use (which I call dream boards) are the start of your work, not the end of it. You create and keep these visual reminders around so that you are constantly aware of what you're working toward. They're not a security blanket. They're not a sweet little daydream about what might someday happen if you just hope and wish hard enough. They're a kick in the butt. They're a call to action. And when you mess up and fall on your ass—because you *will* mess up and fall on your ass—they remind you why you're going to get back up and get moving in the right direction again.

Throughout all of this, you've still got your declaration drawn out on a piece of paper or pinned up to a board or however you've done it. Remember, your declaration is your twenty-year plan, and it literally can be as simple as the crayon drawing I did when I was a kid. The sixty-six-day boards are where you get into detail, where you really break it down. The sixty-six-day boards have a specific function—they keep you on track for whatever your current theme is. Your overall declaration doesn't change, but your sixty-six-day board changes with each new theme. And when you're closing out one sixty-six-day theme, the next one will arise. You'll know it because you'll be in tune with what you need to do next.

Partnerships

I just can't stress this enough: You can't do this stuff alone. Structuring your environment is vital to your success, but it doesn't work well if it's the only thing you've got in your corner. Human relationships hold us accountable and make us more successful. Let's say you and your spouse both want to lose weight. If you do it together, you're more likely to lose the weight and keep it off. Or you could try a sixty-six-day theme with one of your kids—I love doing this, because you can really see your relationship grow. It's good for your kids to see you challenged at something, and I believe it's good for them to see you fail, too. Why? Because they see you get back up and start over. "Hey, Dad messed up; he just ate a cupcake, and we're cutting out sugar for sixty-six days." That's okay. Kids are constantly failing and they feel bad about it, so if they see you failing but trying again and not beating yourself up, they learn that the appropriate response to failure is to get your butt back in the game. When you mess up, you don't quit, you just acknowledge your mistake and get back on track. That is a powerful example to set.

So, spouses and kids are terrific accountability partners. Coaches and groups are great for this, too. Let's say you're training for a race. If you can find a running team that trains together, that level of accountability will have you hitting the road to get those miles in more efficiently than if it's just you yelling at yourself to do it.

When Dawn was running half marathons, she had training partners. And they kept each other on track, constantly checking in with each other. "Did you get in your ten miles today?" "No, I didn't. Want to run with me tomorrow?" They kept each other accountable.

With Axel, we had two recent reminders of how important partnerships can be. He was sent to a physical therapist, and instead of doing the normal thing and having only me or Dawn go with him to the PT appointment, we walked in there with me, Dawn, Axel, and Axel's coach, who was a former speed and conditioning coach for several NFL teams and for an Olympic gold medalist. So we could see the physical therapist thinking, *What the heck is going on here?* Axel's coach, who is a really smart guy, said, "Look, we're not here to tell you how to do your job. We're here because we want to make our decisions based on twenty, thirty, forty years into the future. We're talking about the highest levels of athleticism. So we want you to be aware of that and to give him PT based on the future, not based on today. We're not interested in getting him back on the field today." She totally changed her attitude in that moment. She was thinking, *Okay, this kid has to use these legs in an athletic arena for the next thirty years. I'm not going to run him through the usual evaluations and exercises, ice his knee, and send him home.* I really believe he got a different level of care because we were looking so far out into the future.

The same thing happened with the doctor. The doctor examined Axel and said, "Yeah, we could push him through. He's going to play with some pain, and he may lose some biomechanics and some athleticism. He may need to have a surgery, but we can get him through this season." And we said, "Look, he's in sixth grade. We don't care about this season. We care about the season thirty years from now." When he heard that, the doctor reassessed his own decision and said, "Well, then, let's let him heal and get him healthy."

Those things happened for two reasons: Axel has a twenty-year plan, and he has partnerships. And the partnerships he has with us actually brought about a different quality of care with his doctor and with his physical therapist. We told them about Axel's dream, about why we're planning so far into the future, and they stepped up to be part of that dream. They adjusted their recommendations and their treatments because they became partners in Axel's dream.

Schedule Your Championships

The final part of accountability is measurement, or what I call *scheduling your championship*. It's like scheduling an exam. What keeps you ultimately accountable is measurement of your progress. Professional sports teams are really great at this. At the start of the season, you haven't seen each other for months, and all your teammates are there watching you get measured and tested. Your teammates all want to win a championship just like you do, and they're looking at you while you get your speed, your strength, your muscle body mass, and your weight taken and written down. You don't want to be embarrassed in front of your peers, so you're going to show up fast and in shape and lean and tough.

Now, if you're like most people, you aren't on a sports team, but you still need measurements and tests. You still need to know that you're improving. So you have to schedule your own championships.

Let's stick with the sports analogy for a moment. Let's say your twenty-year declaration is to be the best runner. You need to schedule championships along the way, and you decide to run the LA Marathon. This race is usually held in March, so you start planning for race day six months ahead of time. You know what has to happen on October 10. You know what you'll be doing on January 23. Every day of that six months, you know what you have to do. You know what you're going to eat, how far you've got to run that day, what sort of other workout is necessary. Months before the marathon is run, you sit down and you plot out your training. That act of committing to running a marathon dictates what has to happen today, and what has to happen in thirty days, and in sixty days, and every day in between.

Once you make a commitment like this, especially if you make it really specific like *I'm going to run this marathon in under three hours,* then your ass is on the line. You cannot be casual about it any longer.

To meet that goal, you have to reverse engineer your way forward. You're going to plan your runs, your speed workouts, your weight-room sessions. If you need them, you're going to schedule in massages or PT sessions. You're going to plan what you eat. You're going to plan how much sleep you get. And you're going to have that all planned out for months in advance.

Along the way, you're constantly measuring: How

much faster have I gotten? What's my per-minute pace on my long runs? How much more efficient is my running? Am I eating well? Am I feeling healthy and rested? Is this a recovery day?

Inside that six-month training period, you'll have several sixty-six-day chunks of time to use however you think best. Maybe for the first sixty-six days, you fine-tune your nutrition and figure out how best to support your body with food. Maybe then your body tells you that the next sixty-six days need to focus on correcting a stride issue or pay more attention to rubbing down your feet and legs. You'll know what to work on if you just stay in tune with your body.

Once you plan that training period, you've built an environment that totally supports you. You're going after this championship, and you've put an environment in place that saves you a ton of energy. You're basically painting by numbers, connecting the dots, when you've got this all laid out. You expend very little energy thinking about what to do because you've already figured out what you need to do every single day. So there's no thought involved, no decisions to make. You just do what your plan tells you to do, and you take constant measurements to see how you're progressing.

Push this idea out into the longer term, and you'll see how it can profoundly change your life. You keep planning out sixty-six-day chunks of your life, and all of a sudden, you're two years into your declaration and you've changed. Your body starts to react to what's necessary for you to be the best in twenty years. You get lean; you get efficient; you sleep better. You're not getting distracted anymore because everything is all planned out for you.

Now, this should be obvious, but I'm going to say it anyway. You're not going to improve if you keep doing the same thing in the same way. You'll make a habit after sixty-six days, yeah, but you won't necessarily be any better at it when that time period is up.

To improve, you have to practice beyond your comfort zone.

Anders Ericsson calls this *practicing outside your current capacity*. Remember his theory that you need ten thousand hours of deliberate, focused practice to become an expert at something? In his most recent book, *Peak: Secrets from the New Science of Expertise*, he takes that idea even further. If your current sixty-six-day plan is to run a certain number of miles each day, great. Go for it. But if you want to get faster, just running those miles at the same rate every day won't help you speed up. You have to increase your effort and practice outside your comfort zone. That's the only way to improve.

Think about it. If you commit to running three miles every day for sixty-six days, and every day you run at a nine-minute-per-mile pace, at the end of those sixty-six days, you'll be running at a nine-minute-per-mile pace. So while that's great—you ran three miles a day for sixty-six days!—you haven't really improved. You haven't gotten faster. You're not going to go run a 5K and smash a record. Why? Because you haven't been training outside your capacity. You haven't been pushing yourself.

Another thing to keep in mind is that after a certain number of hours of deliberate, focused practice, you reach a place that Ericsson calls the *point of no return*. No one can catch up to you at that point, which is around seventeen thousand hours. Once you hit that seventeen thousand hours of focused, committed, boundary-pushing practice, you are uncatchable.

Axel is focused on becoming uncatchable. When he declared he wanted to play in both the NBA and the NFL, we knew we needed a plan for him to get there. So we reverse engineered that plan over fifteen years. He made his declaration at age six, and he'll be drafted out of college into the pros around age twenty-one. We worked backward from that and said, "How many hours of training per day will it take for you to be the greatest athlete in the world when you leave college?" We figured out that it would be about four hours a day. And at that rate, he'll reach close to twenty-four thousand hours of practice when he hits twenty-one. No other kid his age will be able to touch him at that point, unless some other eleven-year-old is doing what he's doing right now.

Here's a current example of being uncatchable. Why does Brazil's team dominate the men's soccer world? Probably because Brazilian boys play soccer from a really young age. They play without equipment. They play without decent fields. Some of them play barefoot. They play constantly because soccer is woven into the heart of

Brazilian culture. Younger kids go up against older kids; they learn to be really creative at moving the ball because they know they're going to get smacked if they hold on to the ball too long.

By the time these boys are around thirteen years old, they've not only gotten in around ten thousand hours of soccer playing time; they've also played outside their capacity during most of those hours. They are constantly having to improve to stay in the game. By contrast, English boys who are also seriously committed to the sport of soccer reach ten thousand hours of playing time at about twenty-three years old.

Any question why Brazil's men regularly kick butt on the soccer field? It's all right there in the numbers. Starting at a young age, those kids play, and they make mistakes, and they get trampled on by older, better players, and they learn how to do things differently, and the next day they show up at the field and they play again. And after thousands of hours, they're uncatchable.

Your Mind-Set—in an Airtight Container

What happens when we slip up? I mean, we can't stay on course 100 percent of the time. What can we do to get back on track?

Kellyann Petrucci is the *New York Times* bestselling author of *Dr. Kellyann's Bone Broth Diet: Lose Up to 15 Pounds, 4 Inches—and Your Wrinkles!—in Just 21 Days.* She has worked with me for years and explained an excellent tool to keep her mind-set on track:

There isn't any reason why I've accomplished so much. I'm an average girl from nowhereville. My father was a barber. When I started out, I had no connections. I had no ins. I had no money. I didn't have anything other than passion and drive, and I needed to find people who could help me level up. So I studied in Europe, then I became a clinician with a successful practice. People responded well to the Swiss medicine that I practiced. They found it intriguing and appealing, which led me to write my first of five books.

Eventually, I got to a point where I was ready to take my success to a new level, and that brought me to Bo. The first time I heard him talk, I felt as if he were speaking only to me. He had that way of speaking and connecting. What I learned from him, and keep learning, was that we should go for greatness, and to do that, we must hold a mind-set that's different from most people. That mind-set is the decision to be great.

Working with Bo, I started getting to the next level. It happened because I worked hard, and I held that mind-set airtight. The more you create that pathway, the more things happen that you just can't explain. Then when things are dark, and they always become dark at some point, you can flip that switch back much more quickly than you ever could before. When things go wrong or get disappointing, you can't go into that dark hole that some people go into when they get sidetracked. I've found that when I keep myself in Bo's mind-set, more things come my way. When things don't turn out how I expect, I stay in that space of expecting greatness. When you do this, you actually start developing that muscle of, *Wow, good things happen when I do this.* And it becomes normal for you. Your body literally creates a pathway for greatness. Just like when you exercise, you create muscle memory, when you keep Bo's mind-set every day, you create a new habit.

Check out Kellyann's website at www.drkellyann.com.

Fall Down, Get Up

A while back, Axel was in the middle of sixty-six days of not eating sugar. He was so committed. We were so proud of him. This sixty-six-day period fell right into the holiday season, which we knew would be pretty hard on him. Dawn and I decided to show up at his school Christmas party, thinking we'd surprise him with some sugar-free hot chocolate and sugar-free cookies. We figured it would be easier on him if he could have his own treats instead of feeling left out of all the food fun around his classmates.

So we walked up to the school with all these sugar-free goodies for him. His class was outside decorating cookies. We spotted Axel off in the distance, and I am not kidding you, he was head-down in the cookies and the frosting and the jelly beans. He lifted his head, and his face was literally covered in sugar. And he just looked at us, and his whole face was like, *Noooo, not my parents!*

It was so funny. And at the same time, we could see how disappointed in himself he was. But we just said to him, "Axel, that's part of the game. That's part of winning. That frosting on your face? Just wipe it off, and let's start again. Don't beat yourself up. We're not perfect either. We fail all the time."

That's what becoming the best is all about. We hold the intent. We hold the dream. And when we mess up, we stand back up, and we recommit to the intent and to the dream. There's nothing shameful about failing. There's only shame in not getting back up.

I really believe that shame is the death of all dreams. Fortunately for me, I don't respond to failure with shame. When I mess up, I just right the ship and get back on course.

If there's one thing I want you to take away from this chapter, it's to realize that the only way to improve is to fail, to be off course. Of course, first you need to know what it means to be on course. So get that figured out. And then get out there and fail. Because you will fail, over and over. But if you have your course plotted out, you have something to come back to.

Most people are so embarrassed by failure and so ashamed of themselves that they won't even participate. They never get started because they're afraid they'll mess up. Well, if you don't participate, you don't improve. It's that simple. So get over it, get over yourself, and get in the game.

One final thing: No matter how old you are, it's never

too late to start living this way. I'll be close to sixty by the time this book is published, and I'm starting on a new declaration while I'm writing this book. Why the hell not? I'll be seventy-eight years old someday; I might as well spend the time between now and then getting really good at doing something new.

If you're older, you might be telling yourself, *I'll never reach ten thousand hours of practice.* That might be true. But you could reach four thousand hours or six thousand hours of really serious, committed practice—practice that is performed outside your current capacity. Imagine how deeply that would change your life. You could train yourself to push really hard in pursuit of your goal. You could build an environment that supports you and create supportive partnerships and run races or write books or sail oceans that you never imagined you'd see. Only one thing is certain: You won't do any of that if you don't plan for it and then put your foot on the path. What the hell are you waiting for? If you're fifty years old now, you'll be seventy years old in twenty years whether or not you commit to something really exciting.

Don't wait another day. Commit now.

ACTION STEPS

1. Schedule a championship—something you can commit to and measure. This is where the sixty-six-day challenge works really well. Whether you commit to running a race, or getting up an hour

earlier every day to work out, or learning a new skill that will help you succeed in your job, or losing a set amount of weight in sixty-six days, or whatever is meaningful for you, schedule the championship and measure your achievement when the challenge is over.

2. Create a team so you can hold each other accountable. Train together, write together, commit to a shared theme, and check in each day.

Download your free calendar to schedule your championship and plan your sixty-six-day challenge at boeason.com/actionsteps. You can also find examples of our own sixty-six-day challenges here.

8.

RE-COMPETE

Remember my story from earlier about Axel's basketball team and how horrifically bad they were? Hands down, they were the worst team in the league. They didn't quit, though. Instead, they worked long and hard to improve, practicing outside their comfort zone every time they got on the court. And once they started winning, the best players from other teams joined Axel's team, and now these kids are unbeatable.

Sounds great, right? Actually, not so much. A lot of the thrill has gone out of the game for them. Their rate of improvement is not as steep because they're not being challenged. They're not forced to practice beyond their current capacity. They're not really competing. They're not even having very much fun; it's boring to know you're always going to wipe the floor with your opponents.

Likewise, it's demoralizing to know that you're going

to lose, and lose badly, if one team is just plain un-beatable. And there's a certain shame in being handed a trophy at the end of the season even if you hardly ever played, much less won anything. There's no growth in the whole "participation trophy" view of kids' sports. Ask any kid. If they win a championship or a league title, they're going to value that trophy. That trophy means something. It's going on the mantel or on top of their bookcase or somewhere prominent. Otherwise, unless they're really young kids and it's their first year or two of playing on a team, the trophies don't mean much. Just like us, kids need to grow competitively. They need areas in their lives where they can compete and fail and get up and start over and get better. They need to keep growing. And without challenge, without competition, they won't grow.

This sort of thing is happening on the pro level, too. We'll never know how spectacular some of these professional players could be, because they're not truly challenging themselves. If they won't compete, they won't improve. We all lose when this happens.

Somewhere along the way, we've let go of the idea that competition is a noble and innately human drive. We routinely ask less of ourselves than we can give. We're ashamed to be competitive; it's even used as a put-down. "Oh, you're so competitive." You can hear exactly how that comment sounds, can't you? It sure isn't delivered in an admiring tone of voice. It's a modern insult, because in our culture, competitive people are perceived as being pushy and self-centered and uncaring.

Businesspeople are routinely asked to sign non-compete clauses when they start a job. Why the hell would you do that? I was asked to sign one of those, and it made no sense to me. I'm a competitor. Competing is as natural to me as breathing. And I'm convinced you're the same way, even if you've covered up that part of yourself.

Nurturing Competition—by . . . Mom

My parents, Marilyn and Chaz Eason, raised us six children on a ranch in Northern California and instilled a passion for hard work and excellence in all of us. Competition was as natural as breathing. "They are all over-achievers," Marilyn says. "Dealing with six of them was not the easiest chore in the world. All of them were three-sport athletes. Sometimes people would say to me, 'Your kids are only interested in sports,' and I'd say, 'Well, at least they're not roaming the streets getting into trouble.'

"All six of my children are competitive. And I think that's good. It's competitive to breathe. From the day you're born, you're competing for something. That's always been my attitude, and I passed it on to my children. They're all such hard workers and always have been. They weren't spoiled—well, Bo's sisters spoiled him because he was the cutest little kid ever. But we made sure they worked hard, especially in the summers, so they'd know they needed a college education. They either worked as farm or ranch labor or in the feed plant Chaz managed or in the pear orchards. Bo had a friend whose father owned a bait shop, and each summer, Bo and his friend caught crawdads and sold them to his friend's dad, and that was his summer job. They set traps out in the river, and every morning they got in the boat and emptied the traps. Hopefully, there were crawdads in there, because those boys depended on that money."

My granddad, Mom's father, was a football coach in addition to being a United Service Organizations manager during World War II, so Mom came by her love of sports and hard work naturally. "My family was very poor while I was growing up, even though my dad was a college graduate. We moved to a lot of different army and air force bases. I went to eight different high schools. And even though I hated every single second of moving all the time, when I look back on it now, I think things were so good, because it helped me learn how to deal with different types of people. I just didn't know it at the time."

Mom and Dad were completely focused on us as kids and supported us in everything we did or wanted to do. She says, "My husband used to tell them, 'You're the best in there.' He always said, 'Even if they turn out to be cheerleaders, I'll be there in the stands backing them up.' We really believed that if your child has a wish or a dream, you should encourage it, no matter what it is. I know how we raised our kids is not everybody's way, but it was our way. Some parents, I think, are more interested in their lifestyle than in their children. I'm not sure how to put this, but we didn't go to adult parties. We would go to a ball game instead. The kids came first."

Putting the kids first may be why Mom spotted my

early single-minded focus on a goal. "Bo had such determination growing up. He and his brother threw balls
around all the time, even inside the house. Many lamps
were broken! He fought hard for what he got, because he
wasn't as big as most ball players. I mean, he was eighty-
nine pounds when he went to high school. But he ran
faster than lightning, so I thought that would help him,
and it did. I don't think anyone could have talked him
down from his goal of playing in the NFL. We certainly
encouraged him all the way. We knew he was good, because everyone had seen him play in high school, but they
didn't think he'd ever go beyond that. In fact, in high
school, he won the all-league offense and defense awards.
The coaching staff decided he didn't need two trophies,
so they gave the defense trophy to someone else. We knew
how good he was, and that's what mattered."

Mom knows about the current health concerns about
long-term brain damage from head injuries received in
contact sports, especially football, and she understands
that some parents choose to opt their children out of such
sports. But she cautions parents not to fret too much.
"Some parents don't want their kids to play football because they're afraid something will happen. Well, things
happen to your kids. Believe me, both of my boys had
concussions. You sit there and hold your breath. It's just
what you do. But you never tell them that.

"Bo had six knee surgeries, and I sat there with him
through all six of them. I didn't particularly want him to
go on. It's not much fun sitting in the grandstand or in

front of your television and watching your kid play football because of all the injuries. But I never told him that. After his sixth knee surgery, he told me, 'I've had enough.' I never told him to quit. He had to be the one to say it. I had faith in his dream and in his decision, whatever it was."

After I left football, Mom and Dad had faith in me when I decided to become an actor and playwright, as well. The intensely personal nature of *Runt of the Litter* led some people to wonder how the play would be received by my family. Mom just shrugs off any hint of family conflict. "We knew what was true and what was not true in his play. He used to have a question-and-answer time after the play. And one night we were there, and a person in the audience asked, 'How do your parents take this criticism? Are they angry with you?' He said, 'Well, gee, I don't know. When I got here to the studio, my dad was sweeping the stage off for me.'"

The Attractiveness of Competition

When I was growing up, I loved watching professional boxing, especially Muhammad Ali and Joe Frazier. Ali was the heavyweight champion of the world, and he fought all the other heavyweight greats. It seemed like he had major matches once a month. I fell in love with boxing because of the competition and the tension; these guys gave it everything they had. And as a result, the sport of boxing got better. It got bigger and more competitive and produced incredible fighters. Not anymore. Now, the best won't fight the best, because it's not good for them financially if they lose. As a result, the sport has declined because of the lack of competition and the lack of conflict.

Competition and conflict make sports compelling. Sports events get their highest ratings when they showcase gladiators who are wholeheartedly competing against one another. Without those two attributes, and without the structure that allows for competition, you just have a bunch of really talented people who are wasting their time and ours. If all the best people join one team, there's no more competition. If safety regulations go so far that the game is no longer recognizable, there's no more competition. Who wants to watch a boring game that's held back and diminished by the referees and the rule book instead of being driven by the players?

This holds true in sports, in business, in life. In his book *Peak,* Anders Ericsson said that the only fields that his theory of deliberate practice doesn't apply to are those fields in which there is little or no direct competition. Jobs such as engineer, business manager, consultant, or electrician have no objective criteria for superior performance because there's no direct competition. So our society gets weaker in those areas rather than better, because competition makes us better.

Imagine Usain Bolt without someone nipping at his heels. He's going to run fast enough to beat the next fastest guy, no matter how fast that guy is. That's competition. He's faster because other people are forcing him to be faster than they are.

The day I'm writing this, Eliud Kipchoge of Kenya smashed the world marathon record at the Berlin Marathon. He finished in less than two hours and two minutes—more than a minute faster than the previous world record. And as he ran the last couple of hundred meters toward the Brandenburg Gate and the finish line, he was running flat out. You'd never guess he'd been going for more than twenty-six miles. The guy was sprinting, and there was no one near him. He was competing against the rest of the field, yeah, but at the end, he was only competing against himself. Nobody could have over-taken him. He could have slowed down. He didn't.

In their book *The Lessons of History*, Will and Ariel Durant make the argument that the laws of biology underlie the fundamental lessons of history. And the very first biological law is that life is competition: "Competi-tion is not only the life of trade, it is the trade of life—peaceful when food abounds, violent when the mouths outrun the food. Animals eat one another without qualm; civilized men consume one another by due process of law. Co-operation is real, and increases with social develop-ment, but mostly because it is a tool and a form of com-petition; we co-operate in our group—our family, our community, our club, church, party, 'race,' or nation—in order to strengthen our group in competition with other groups."

Think about that for a minute. Competition is the life of trade and the trade of life. Cooperation is actually a form of competition because it makes your group stronger than the group down the road. Competition is who we are; it's how we're created; it's literally in our DNA.

Unfortunately, a current trend toward victimhood totally undermines this fundamental human law. People are trying to get ahead by claiming that they're victims of society rather than fully functioning members. And yet we all have the same biological makeup. We're all competitive beings. That's simply how we're created.

The really great competitors have figured this out. If there's no competition for themselves, they create it. Baryshnikov, Michael Jordan, Usain Bolt get to a point where they're looking around for some competition, for someone to test themselves against, and they can't find it. So they innately know that they have to compete against themselves.

This is how it worked for me. I wanted to be the best stage performer in the world, and then the best speaker in the world, and now I'm at a point where I look around and I think, *Well, shit, that's who I am. Now what?*

I'm competing against my last performance, is what. I used to be able to compete in a game that has been around professionally for nearly a hundred years. I measured myself against every man who had ever played safety on any team during that entire century. I knew exactly how I measured up against the best players. I made myself better, I made the game a little better, and some safety who follows me will make it better because he saw me play and decided to be better than I was. I love that. That's how it's supposed to work.

My daughter Eloise is determined to be the best performer, whether a pastry chef or Broadway actress. She's set on that goal and is putting all the foundations in place to bring it to life. At a certain point, many years from now, she'll be competing against herself, against her last performance. Can she go deeper into the part? Can she be better with this piece of dialogue? Can the blocking of the play improve, the movement, the precision? All these things become really fine measurements once you reach the top, but to improve and not just phone it in, you have to keep measuring yourself and challenging yourself to do better.

Competition always brings out the best in us. It raises the standard. If you couldn't win a gold medal for high jump, how high do you think people would be jumping? Why would they compete if there's no competition, unless they're the best and they're competing against themselves? Would they be throwing themselves eight feet into the air if there were not a way to measure that jump?

Measurements and scores help you be a true competitor. Competition against other greats makes you a better competitor. If you stop demanding more of yourself than you can currently give—if you stop practicing outside your current capacity—your competitive nature dies. You stop improving. Imagine that degradation taking place across an entire sport; the sport itself goes downhill. Across an entire culture, the entire culture goes downhill.

I was lucky heading into the NFL. I knew exactly who

I was chasing and who I wanted to learn from and eventually unseat—Mike Reinfeldt on the Houston Oilers. Here's a great example of how competition is not an ugly, hate-filled thing. I respected Mike more than any other NFL player. I wanted to be him! And when I finally beat him out, that was just nature following its course. That's how it's supposed to go.

Just like I modeled myself on Mike and I sought out Al Pacino, you need to find the person who is the best in your chosen field. Study them. Meet with them if you can. Learn from them; compete with them; take their advice wherever you can find it. And when you work hard enough and finally beat them out—and you will beat them out if you do what I'm telling you to do—then you'll be competing against yourself.

This whole process is about making yourself the best in the world so that future generations will have someone to compete against. They'll have a way to measure themselves and a standard to hold themselves up to. That's a truly worthwhile legacy for you to leave behind.

There's Honor in Failing

I know you're thinking, *What the heck, Bo? What about the idea about becoming the best? Why would I even consider failing?*

You should consider failing because you are going to fail often. Get used to it. Failure is going to make you better. We really hate to fail, I know. But this process of competing will require that you lose most of the time.

That's hard to accept. Sometimes when we lose, we tell ourselves we're no good, we're not worth improving, we don't matter. Nothing could be further from the truth. You just need to reframe how you think about failure.

I've mentioned this several times already, but it's at the core of how you're going to live your life, so it bears repeating. You are going to be off course 99 percent of the time. That's because you're human. Get over that fear of failure. Embrace failure as an opportunity to learn, get back up, and kick butt another day. No drama, just action.

Similarly, you will have times in your life where you have to choose between development and winning. Always choose development! You should be making your decisions based on long-term, not short-term, thinking. You want to always be thinking twenty years into the future. Make friends with your future self. Ask your future self, *What's the best decision for me to make right now?* Your future self won't let you down; it will always opt for long-term goals instead of instant gratification.

Here's an example. Let's say you have a chance to play a part where your entire role is to walk onstage, put down a vase of flowers, and then leave the stage, but you get to share the stage with Al Pacino for those three seconds. And you get to do that for an entire year. Or you could take a role where you're the lead and you're the best actor in the play.

I'd take the silent role that is onstage with Al Pacino for three seconds, and here's why. You put me around that dude for a year, and I'm going to sponge everything he knows. I'm going to watch him from the wings. I'm going to watch him during rehearsal. I'm going to study his every move, his line readings, the changes he suggests, how he moves his body, how he interacts with not just the other actors but with the space around him. That's development. I will choose development over winning every time.

Or let's say one of your challenges right now is that you've gained some weight, you've slowed down, you're not as fit as you used to be. If you ask your today self whether you should park your butt on the couch with a bag of chips and a beer while you watch TV or whether you should drink a glass of water and head outside for some sweaty exercise, your today self is going to be laughing its head off and tossing you the TV remote. Ask your future self. Ask your twenty-years-from-now self what your best choice is, and I can guarantee you'll find yourself outside, ready to go, before you know what's happened.

That's the power of having a long-term declaration. You don't have to make any decisions today, because you already know what you're doing. You just follow your declaration and your plan. You're thinking twenty years into the future. It's simple.

That's how we're raising our kids. Right now, we want Axel to develop as an athlete. We don't care if he wins. As a competitor, yeah, I want him to win, and he wants to win, but he's only in the sixth grade. Development is key for him. A lot of coaches, even in these younger age groups, will sacrifice the development of a player to get a victory. I always opt the opposite way. I'd rather lose and take the pain of losing but learn something and grow from the experience.

That's honorable. That's an honest way of going through life. That's the life I committed to years ago.

In Shakespeare's *Henry V,* the king of France, Charles VI, tries to avoid war with England by offering Henry his daughter Catherine in marriage and a few small dukedoms. Henry responds:

> *I am not covetous for gold*
> *Nor care I who doth feed upon my cost;*
> *It yearns me not if men my garments wear;*
> *Such outward things dwell not in my desires.*
> *But if it be a sin to covet honor,*
> *I am the most offending soul alive.*

In my life, it seems that development equals honor equals earning your victories. Losing is honorable if you've given 100 percent of what you have. I prefer that to winning but asking less of yourself. In my mind, that's not honorable. That's not how you become a better person. Henry turned down the chance to walk away from war with a new wife, some French lands, and a couple of worthless titles because he believed he was in the right; he believed his honor was at stake. And, against what should have been insurmountable odds, his belief carried him to victory.

Your belief will do the same for you.

Stay with Me Here

I know I've thrown a lot at you in this chapter, and some of it might not sit well with you. I get that. This stuff is hard, and it's counter to today's culture, and you might not agree with how I feel. But I'm asking you to just stick with me because I can promise that if you do, you'll reclaim your natural self. I'm asking you to do it because I've done it myself. I know what it takes. I know it's possible.

And I know that once you make your declaration and do what I do, do what my family does, do what my clients do, you're going to reach the top of your chosen field. You will. There's no doubt in my mind. No one else is going to compete as hard or as smart as you. You will be unstoppable.

Once you're alone at the top, you'll push yourself to keep improving because you'll be used to functioning like the competitive human being you are. Living like that will be ingrained habit many years before you reach your declaration.

One final thought: If you compete in a world that won't compete, guess who becomes extremely valuable and exceedingly attractive?

That's right. You do.

One final word before we get to the action step—as you head for the top of your field, you may find yourself more alone in your success than you'd expected. You've made sacrifices along the way; you're reduced distractions; you've probably alienated people who weren't helping you move forward to your declaration. Lauren Holiday describes it this way:

It's lonely being on the road, because only certain people understand what you're going through, and those people are your teammates. I have a childhood friend who isn't on the national team, and I remember her telling me, "Just because you're doing this doesn't mean you can ignore me."

And I thought, *Wow, she's so right.* But it's easy to ignore people who don't understand what I'm going through. And not just ignore them—not invest in those relationships at all because it's easier to stay uninvolved than to try to explain your lifestyle. But as a result, you feel isolated, and only a small percentage of people understand what you're doing, or why you're sacrificing what you sacrifice, or why you're working toward what you're working toward. And the more successful you get, the more lonely the lifestyle is.

And on the other hand, you find yourself surrounded by only those people who believe in you and your dream. It's your choice.

ACTION STEPS

1. Name your areas of success. Where in your life do you have freedom and success and happiness and a sense of achievement? You know where; it's where you're competing. It's the place where you live most fully, like a little neighborhood of your life. It might be your career, your ability to make money, what a great parent you are, or how much love and nurturing you deliver to those around you. Those are the areas where you make yourself better every single day because you're competing with yourself to continually do better. You have a lot of freedom in those places, a lot of self-worth, a lot of success.

2. Now identify the places in your life where you're not competing—the things you're not so great at. I guarantee you you're not competing in those areas. You're not accessing your innate competitive spirit. In those areas, you're living as if you're entitled to a victory. You're acting like you're not allowed to lose—if you don't compete, you can't lose, right? I want you to dig out those areas because they're holding you back. Stop avoiding competition. Look for it. Embrace it. Make yourself play a bigger game.

3. Get comfortable with the idea of failure. You're not going to become the best by playing it safe and

avoiding risks, so test yourself against the best competitors you can find. Stick with the hard stuff. Fall down and get back up. Remember, difficulty forces you to stretch and compete outside your current capacity. Failure helps you grow.

9.

DISTRACTIONS

We live in the most distracted time in human history. That probably doesn't surprise you. Smartphones, computers, tablets, texting, surfing the web, social media, email alerts, everything on demand ... we're all more distracted than we were twenty, or even ten, years ago. I feel pretty strongly about staying on course, as you know, and I don't very often get pulled into the vast hole of time-suck that is the internet. But a few days ago, I was poking around on Facebook, and my phone popped up a text message alert. It took me a moment to realize that I was actually being distracted from my distraction. I course-corrected but got a good laugh at myself.

Distraction surrounds us. I rarely go to regular gyms, but I do have a membership at a nice, new gym close to our home. The first time I walked in there, though, I counted twenty-four big-screen TVs near the treadmills.

Big-screen TVs were lined up in front of the stationary bikes, too. And as if that weren't enough, each of the treadmills and bikes had its own little TV built right into it. That told me that this gym is not really about working out. It's about distracting yourself long enough to get through a treadmill run or a bike ride.

The best do not do that. The best actually do what they do. If they're exercising, they focus on exercising, on how their bodies are working, on what muscles are being engaged. They don't distract themselves with electronics. They're actually showing up to their practice. How the hell do you practice outside your current capacity if you're not paying attention? You can't. A distracted practice session might keep you from losing ground, but it's not going to make you healthier or move you closer to your declaration. If you're truly practicing outside your comfort zone, you're struggling too much to be distracted. It takes maximum effort, and everything else falls away.

I'm not the only one who's noticed this high level of distraction, of course. Cal Newport, in his book *Deep Work,* writes, "The ability to perform deep work is becoming increasingly rare at exactly the same time it is becoming increasingly valuable in our economy. As a consequence, the few who cultivate this skill, and then make it the core of their working life, will thrive."

So you can bemoan the current state of our culture, or you can see it for what it truly is: a huge opportunity. If we live in the most distracted time in human history, let's take advantage of that. Let's capitalize on that distracted world. This is a fabulous way to compete. It's a way to fly in the face of the culture, which you know I encourage. While most of the world is becoming increasingly distracted, texting as they walk and falling off curbs into oncoming traffic, and mistaking electronic blips on a screen for true connection, a select few are capitalizing on this huge cultural shift. That's us. We're part of that small group going in the opposite direction of everyone else. They can be as distracted as they want. We're choosing instead to focus.

The culture we have to go out there and create in is incredibly distracted. We can create our environment to a certain extent. We can eliminate as many distractions as possible. But we cannot take away all distractions. So you have to learn how to dance with some of them.

You know by now that nothing I suggest comes without a lot of work. If you make the choice to focus, it will take concentration and commitment. It is a choice to break the habit of being distracted. The only way to do so is to remember that you are playing a bigger game with a longer-term goal. Unless your dream is a bigger game than the distractions you face every day, you won't fulfill your declaration.

I've already discussed how if you build your environment right, you don't have to lean on your own willpower so much. One of the environment-building things we've done for our kids is to limit their access to electronics. We know, for instance, that if Axel has a phone, that thing is going to take over his life. Axel does not have a phone.

And we're not alone in this conviction. Bill and Melinda Gates, for instance, didn't let their kids have cell phones until they were fourteen years old. Steve Jobs similarly banned his kids from having cell phones when they were young. What do these people who built our current tech-obsessed world know that we don't? They know that electronics are hugely addictive. They know that they want something different, something better, for their own kids. So they protect their kids.

Who's protecting your kids from distraction? Who's protecting you? For your entire family, ask, *What are we hearing, how are we being herded, how are we being deliberately manipulated and distracted? And how do we protect from distraction?* Protecting your time and your mental state is incredibly important. Let's say you're deep in the zone, possibly writing or concentrating closely on something. Now, if someone walks in and asks you a question, it takes you at least fifteen minutes to get back into the zone. That's not just being interrupted. That's like throwing a bomb into your ability to reach your goal, again and again and again.

Another way to be distracted is to be vulnerable to people telling you, "Oh, that's an impossible goal." Instead of supporting you in your declaration, they put you down. For many of us, that knocks us off course. That sort of input is a huge distraction and worry. You're trying to adopt a professional mind-set, and they're coming at you from an amateurish frame of mind. According to Steven Pressfield, "Amateurs play for fun; pros play for keeps." You're learning how to be a professional. Don't be distracted by the amateurs. Don't give their negativity space in your head. You've got a big job in front of you for the next two decades; don't question your ability, your skill, your commitment, or your drive because someone else can't believe the way you do.

One of my favorite ways to manage distractions is absolutely backward of what you'd think it would be—so again, going counter to the culture—and you can think of it as inclusive distraction.

Here's an example. Let's say a pro basketball player, Kobe Bryant, maybe, is in a high-pressure situation. He's at the free throw line at the end of a game. The game is on the line, there's one second left, he has two free throws that will win the game, but if he misses the shots, they lose. So here's how an amateur mind would handle this situation: *Okay, I've got to completely focus on the basket and on putting the ball in the basket. Everything else is invisible. I've got to have tunnel vision. I'll just focus on the basket, the ball, and me.*

Let's look at what Kobe would do. He gets the ball from the referee with one second on the clock. He's standing there on the free throw line, and as he gets ready to shoot, he includes everything. He includes the guy screaming ten feet away from him, "Miss it, miss it, miss it!" He includes the smell of popcorn inside the sports arena. He includes the sweat dripping down the side of his face. He includes the hundreds of fans sitting behind the basket waving those long, skinny blow-up sticks in the air and shouting at him. It's all part of his world for those moments, and he takes it all in. He includes everything, and then he sinks the ball in the basket.

That is what we call *ultra-presence*. That is doing a dance with everything around you and being inclusive of everything around you. And it's the complete opposite of what amateurs think you should do. Tunnel vision is not the way to go, even if that seems logical or intuitive.

It's not just in sports, of course. I was on a movie set once, and a big star was in front of the cameras shooting a scene. He definitely didn't have tunnel vision. There were about a hundred people standing around. So there was the star, waiting for the cameras to start, and he was surrounded by people. Picture it: There was a guy putting makeup on his foot. A woman was fixing his hair. There was somebody messing with his clothes and making sure his shirt collar was just right; there was a soundman; there was a union worker off to the side having a cigarette. They were all around, and the star had to focus on the scene and then deliver. And I saw him take in the whole crazy scene around him, instead of excluding it, and then deliver the scene. That was true freedom. That was true focus.

Think of a person who has to dance with distraction as a matter of life and death. If you're a Navy SEAL or a Green Beret or a firefighter in the middle of all hell breaking loose, do you think you can afford to be distracted? You're not going to be wondering, *How many likes can I get on Facebook if I post a selfie right now?* or *Man, I hope the Dodgers win tonight.* That's not how these professionals work. They take in all the distractions around them, the bullets and the snipers and the potential bombs, or the flames and the smoke and the yelling, and they dance around those distractions.

They're actually doing what they're doing. They're not capturing what they're doing or planning how they're going to report on what they're doing. They're just doing the thing that's in front of them, the thing they've trained for.

This is how we need to live to fulfill our declaration. We must take our biggest distraction, whatever that monster might be, and name it and get to know it and understand exactly what it is and why it has such a strong hold on us. And then we kill it. But we have to dance around all the other distractions, include them in our planning, and acknowledge that they're part of our day-to-day lives while we get on with creating our dream.

This goes back to building your environment. If you build it correctly, you don't have to rely on your willpower. For instance, if you and I are in the middle of an eleven-mile run, there are not a lot of distractions out there on the road. We're not going to be checking our email or posting to our social media. If we do those things, we're definitely not practicing outside our current capacity; we're just goofing around. Which is fine, on one level. We all need goofing around time. But if you've scheduled a championship, an intermediate goal on the way to your big declaration, then you're going to take your practices seriously, and you're going to train outside your comfort zone. So that pressure itself will help create the environment in which distractions are not as attractive as they once were. If you're serious about your declaration—and I don't know why you've read this far if you're not serious about it—then you know you don't have time to waste.

Ben Hardy on Finding the Advantage

Ben Hardy, author of *Willpower Doesn't Work*, transformed from a difficult childhood—one filled with heavy addiction and pain—into a phenomenally successful adulthood.

"Addiction is such an interesting thing to me," says Hardy. "If you study it, you'll find that willpower does not work with addiction. And we're all addicts when we really look at our behavior. Everything you do is repeated, right? It's all subconscious, so you have to change it as you would an addiction. That was how I approached my book *Willpower Doesn't Work*—how do you make fundamental, permanent change?"

Hardy's answer: You drastically change your environment. His belief comes from his own experience. A year after graduating from high school, he was living at his cousin's house, playing video games for sixteen hours a day, and existing on junk food. He was stuck in an emotional space of sadness and confusion and repetition. "Most people's behavior is exactly what they were doing the day before. They're just repeating subconscious cycles. They're living out their memories. They're not doing anything that's unpredictable or uncertain. But the only way to grow is to shock the subconscious and embrace uncertainty."

Hardy embraced uncertainty by leaving town to work at a humanitarian church-style mission. Immediately, he felt like a light switch had been flipped. "I had a new role, a new identity, and a new perspective. At the end of my time there, my mission leader told me, 'Ben, if you go back home and become the person you were before this experience, that would be the biggest fail.' I came home and nothing in that environment had changed, and I totally felt it. I realized I didn't belong there anymore." Ben left again and created another new environment for himself.

The importance of environment drives Hardy's life and his work. The fact that your current behavior is supported by your environment works in both directions—a positive environment will support positive action; a negative environment, negative action. To live a full life, he believes, we must engage in both high stress (new situations, new challenges) and what he calls *high recovery:*

Recovery is just as important, if not more important, than stress. I'm interested in how refreshed and relaxed people are after they work really hard or work out really hard. If you're always going, going, going, then you can't get better. You're going to be exhausted and depleted. Today's workout will be no better than yesterday's workout, because you're not actually recovered.

Let's say your professional focus is on your sport. If you fill your recovery time with things that truly matter, whether it's your family, or your god, or whatever gives your life great meaning, then you will actually need to spend less time on the sport. The time you spend working will be more purposeful and more productive, because not only will it be enhanced by a good recovery, but it will be enhanced by a higher meaning.

Think about the concept of psychological detachment from work. How much of your time are you actually fully unplugged from your work? For example, if your goal is to spend more time with your family, be really present with them. If you're at the beach with your kid, get in the water and play and goof around. Don't just sit there and read or look at your phone while your kid is in the water.

It's so common for people today to never actually unplug from the network. It's common for people to never fully reengage with their recovery, with the outside world, with friends, with family. But if you don't allow yourself to mentally and emotionally and physically disengage from your job or your work, you burn yourself out. Even if you're performing at what you think is your highest ability, you're actually performing below that, because you're not recovered, you're not engaged.

Ben and his wife have three foster children and are expecting twins. Their time is tight and about to get tighter. Ben views this as an advantage. "I would actually argue that the person with five kids has an advantage over a single, childless person of the same age, because they have such a steep learning curve. If they can optimize their life, they will perform at a higher level, even though they have less free time. In *The Lessons of History,* Will and Ariel Durant wrote, 'The ability of the average man can be doubled if their situation demanded it.' I would rather have a life of meaning and a life of challenge, because that steeper learning curve transfers over to my work."

Ben suggests, especially for parents, to concentrate on the bookends of each day—bookend the evening and morning routines. You can't control how life goes during the day, because a lot of it is controlled by other people or life situations. But your evening and your night and your morning are up to you. Unplug from your technology earlier in the evening and actually be with your kids in a meaningful way. That helps you all have a good evening routine. Your kids can then go to sleep at a decent hour. Then you have the rest of the evening to recover, and you can wake up a little earlier than most people and focus on the challenges of the upcoming day.

Challenge forces you to grow. "What got you where you are isn't what's going to get you to the next place," says Ben. "The brain needs to do new things to thrive. If your growth pattern is steep and you're continually putting yourself in enriched environments, you'll grow a lot. It may feel like crap along the way, but then you'll look back and measure the gains that you've made and you'll be blown away."

And when doubts set in? Ben reminds himself, "God is with me. He's brought me this far. I've watched myself succeed in the past. I'm clear on where I'm going. I know I can get there."

Distractions and the Sixty-Six-Day Themes

The sixty-six-day themes that I discussed in the last chapter will move you toward your declaration. But they have another function: to help you eliminate distractions.

Usually during these sixty-six days, we're working toward something we need to acquire. We might feel that we don't have the capacity we need in a certain area, like the stamina to run a marathon or the ability to write a book. But often we're also eliminating something. For instance, during one of my themes, I stopped drinking wine. I actually did it for more than one hundred days, because once you commit to getting rid of something for sixty-six days, it's not that hard to keep it out of your life. You forget about it, you're not doing it anymore, and you're not distracted by it. So this elimination of distraction actually frees up your time.

If you think you're spending too much time playing video games, try taking that out for sixty-six days and just look at how many more hours you have available during the day. Or if you watch a lot of TV, eliminate that for sixty-six days and then at the end, decide if you want to add it back into your routine. My guess is you won't. I heard recently that North Americans watch something like thirty-four hours of TV every single week. That's nearly the equivalent of a full-time job! If you're watching a lot of TV, don't tell me you don't have time to commit to deliberate practice of some sort or to commit to sixty-six days of eliminating a habit. Drop your TV habit and look at all the time you've just gifted yourself.

I've never been a smoker, but I have heard that the hardest part of quitting smoking isn't actually not smoking. It's the time that you now have on your hands that you used to spend engaging in the ritual of smoking. Think about the steps: You pull out the package, and knock the cigarette out of the package, and get your lighter or your matches, and then you light up and start to smoke. Maybe you have to walk outside if you're at work. That can be a ten-minute ritual from start to finish. If you're a heavy smoker and you smoke fifteen, twenty cigarettes a day, that's a couple of hours every day that you now have at your disposal to do something constructive with.

You no longer have the distraction of your habit, whether it's smoking or playing video games or watching TV or eating junk food. You have a lot of extra time.

So let's talk about the external distractions. The ones we can name, like the internet or TV, are big distractions. We can eliminate that stuff. That's relatively easy. It's the ones you don't even know are distracting you that are so dangerous. You might not think it's a distraction to get a snack, to call a friend, to flip idly through a magazine or social media. You might think of those things as breaks from your routine. I promise you they are distractions, and they are holding you back. You have to be ruthless at digging them out and eliminating them.

The benefits of dropping our distractions are immense, no matter who we are or what we do in life. Most of us aren't going to jump out of an airplane, exchange shots in a firefight with enemy troops, charge into a burning building, or be up on a balance beam at the Olympics. But why don't we put our lives on that balance beam? Why don't we put ourselves figuratively into a firefight and have that same deep practice, that same deep focus? If indeed this is the most distracted time in the world, and it's only going to get worse, why don't we take that situation into our own hands and change things, at least for ourselves and our families?

People are so distracted that they're not asking enough of themselves. Let's turn this global distraction to our advantage. I know that my children are planning to do so. They'll be competing against people their own age who grew up distracted, and because of that, my kids will eventually be competing against themselves.

That's what I want you to do. I want your competitive spirit to be you versus you. Eliminate as much as you can, stomp out your biggest distractions, dance with the ones you can't eliminate, and after that you'll have only yourself to compete against.

I can't stress this enough: You get to decide if you're world-class or not. You get to look at a world that is overrun with distraction, and you get to choose your course of action. You get to say, "I'm not going in that direction.

I'm going in the opposite direction of all the distractions. I'm going toward clarity of purpose. I'm going to capitalize on everyone else's distraction and make it work for me. And one day, they're going to be watching me on TV or cheering as I race in the Olympics or reading my books, and they'll be telling their friends how good I am."

I don't blame anyone for being distracted or think I'm better than they are. Let's face it: This kind of crept up on us over the last quarter century. We're up against huge corporations who have time and money and experts to throw at making sure we stay as distracted as possible, because that's how they make money. The entertainment world is so good. The gaming world is so good. The media is so good. None of these people are stupid. They are top-level at keeping you distracted, at keeping you watching their stuff.

I don't want to watch their stuff. I want to be the person in the arena.

Whenever my kids complain about not playing a video game or not getting to watch huge amounts of TV, I always remind them that their hard work will pay off bigtime because they're not indulging in instant gratification. So my kids might miss some parties with their friends, they might miss a day at an amusement park, but what they will get in the future will be more than worth it.

That's both strange and wonderful when that happens—when the people you went to school with have to pay to watch you do what you do. I grew up surrounded by a lot of guys who were bigger than I was and better athletes than I was. We were in this small town that for some reason just had a shitload of great athletes, and I was not one of them. They knew it, I knew it, and the only thing that put me ahead of them was my ability to keep my future in mind and stay focused on it. I knew that over time, I would catch up to and then pass all these guys who were superior athletes. Why? My declaration most likely put me on a steeper trajectory.

We were all still friends when I started playing pro ball. And I remember one day they came to watch me play. Guess how they got into that stadium? They had to pay for parking, they had to pay for a ticket, they had to pay for a program to watch their old high school chum play pro football. And after the game, I remember this look in their eyes—a numbness, a real regret for what they could have done. I walked out of the locker room, and these very guys who were better than I was, who I had looked up to, were now on the other side of the fence where the fans have to be. And that little shit Bo Eason was on the players' side of the fence.

I walked over to the fence to say hi to my buddies, and I could just see the disillusionment in their faces. *Oh my God, you're that kid who stayed on track. You're the one who kept course-correcting all the time. And I was bigger, faster, and better, but I just stopped, and now I have to pay to see you play.*

That feeling that I had, seeing them like that—it wasn't gloating. It wasn't even a good day for me. It was humbling. I wanted all of them to be with me on the players' side of the fence. I wanted them to be in the locker room with me, because they'd really like it in there. But they couldn't be on the same side I was because they stopped. Maybe they got distracted. Maybe they lost focus, and they didn't get back on track. Maybe they didn't have a Dawn or anyone who believed in them. Maybe it wasn't their dream. Whatever happened, they now had to be on the other side of that fence.

It was hurtful for all of us. It was painful for me to be on this side of the fence and painful for them to be on the other side. And it's a powerful reminder that this is what unchecked distractions look like several decades down the road. It looks like struggle. It looks like exhaustion. It looks like a fan instead of a player.

It looks like regret.

Just thinking back on that, I'm reminded of a Navy SEAL credo, "There are two kinds of pain in the world, the pain of discipline and the pain of regret. You can only avoid one. Choose, O warrior. The decision is always yours."

You can only avoid one of those pains.

I have never, not for a moment, regretted choosing the pain of discipline.

Kevin Ward: Building Your Mental Environment

"I was brought up to believe that it was okay to *do* your best, but the idea of *being* the best at something was too ambitious. It was too self-seeking. It was self-centered. Not only was it unrealistic, but it was also probably evil.

Like you're a bad person if you presume to be the best in the world at something. So that thought just didn't resonate with me," says Kevin Ward. "And then I started working with Bo, and I realized, 'That's my place. That's my responsibility. Not only can I do it, but I am supposed to do it.' Bo opened my eyes to see that what I do matters and that I owe my best to the people I serve."

For twenty years, Kevin was a real estate agent. In 2012, he founded a company that trains real estate agents how to make more money and have a fulfilling life. "Do people selling a home want an agent who's just pretty good? No, they want the best agent who can give them the best result. So I don't train amateurs. I train professionals. I only work with people who are committed to being great at what they do. And that has changed my life completely on the business side. The year before I met Bo, I started my company, and then I lost everything. I'd quit my job, and I wasn't making enough money to make ends meet, and I lost Julie, who's now my wife, and I lost the apartment we lived in. I lost everything except my car and my clothes. I was renting an unfurnished bedroom and sleeping on an air mattress. When I met Bo, things were a little better—I wasn't sleeping on an air mattress anymore—but I was still really struggling. Now we've grown the company to four times what it was making when I met Bo."

Kevin says working with me has changed his personal life just as dramatically. "Now, my goal is not to be a good husband. My goal is to be the best husband in the world, the best friend in the world."

Kevin cautions that this mind-set is not a one-and-done event. "You can't just make a decision: *Okay, I'm going to be the best in the world.* Going from thinking about being pretty good at something to being the best in the world at that thing requires a major shift in the way you approach life. For a long time, my thinking was still mediocre. My thinking was still about being good, not being the best. So I get around Bo as often as I can, because I want to be exposed to his mind-set. That way of thinking, for me, is a major journey."

In the past, Kevin would give himself short-term goals—thirty days, sixty days, a year. For him, the twenty-year time frame that I teach was a huge challenge. "I don't want to wait twenty years! I want fast results. Then I started looking at historical figures who were great leaders and learning how long it took them to actually have major impact. And it was fifteen, twenty, twenty-five years. That helped me realize that this dream of being the best in the world at what I do is not going to happen overnight."

Other methods of mine have also resonated deeply with Kevin. He continually refines his visual representation of his declaration, and he's a dedicated user of the sixty-six-day method of making or breaking a habit. "If I can do something for sixty-six days and create a habit that sets me on a trajectory for the twenty-year plan, that's almost effortless. Really, I've just taken everything Bo's done and tried to implement it in my life. I figure he's a coach, so I'm going to do what he coaches me to do. And then I figure out how to translate that into my world as a coach and help the people I train so they can become the best in the world. I'm always looking for ways to help them think at that level."

Kevin has been in my training and Masterminds for four years and describes himself as a lifer in that program. "Being around Bo elevates me. I go to every Mastermind and every other event that I can. I used to cry every time I'd walk into the Mastermind courses. There would just be tears running down my face, because I was in awe that I was worthy to sit in that room. And I have worked for it. That was my commitment: You tell me what to do, and I'll be your best student. You know how Bo was always the first one to show up at practice and the last one to leave? That's me. I'm the first one to show up for these training events and the last one to leave. Sometimes I'm there before his staff shows up. That's just the way it goes, because that's how he did it, and I'm just doing what Bo does."

Are You in This Video Game? No? Well, Turn It Off

"Hey, Bo! You're on my team!" one of my friends said to me when I was still playing in the NFL.

I had no idea what he was talking about. We didn't play football together. He wasn't even a pro player. Turns out he'd bought one of the John Madden football video games, and I was one of the characters you could choose when you built your team.

I had no idea I'd been put in a game. I didn't know, because I was busy playing the actual game. This came back to me a few years ago when my kids' friends started getting into video games. I really didn't want my kids being distracted with these things, so I made a new family rule: You can only play a game if you're a character in it. And I know other parents think I'm crazy and a little overboard with this stuff, but it works. My kids are not distracted. My kids are not glued to their electronics. My kids are busy doing the things they're passionate about and getting better at them every day. They're busy doing what they do and being fully present. They don't have room for distraction in their lives.

I had a mentor several years ago who said to me, "If you tell me where you're spending your time, I'll tell you your future." He knew the destructive power that unrestrained distractions have on life. Unless an intervention happens, unless you eliminate the distractions you can and learn to dance with the ones you can't eliminate, distractions will run your life.

So which will you choose—the pain of discipline? Or the much deeper pain of regret?

ACTION STEPS

1. What's your biggest distraction? For most of us, it's pretty obvious. Alcohol, TV, video games, social media, snacking—99 percent of you will know what your biggest distraction is. Write it down. Commit to knocking it out as soon as possible. The easiest way to do this is to take sixty-six days and eliminate that sucker. Start today, or tomorrow at the latest.

2. Get your electronic devices out of your life as much as possible. Turn them off. Don't bring them to the dinner table. Give yourself a strict time limit that you can spend on your devices every day and stick to it. Turn off your phone at night.

3. List the distractions that you can't get rid of. You know what they are. Write them down and craft a plan to dance with them, to live with them. You must develop the sort of inclusive focus that a professional athlete or a firefighter has. Accept all the chaos going on around you, and move forward with your focus undisturbed.

4. The most dangerous distractions are the ones you don't even recognize. The best way to uncover them is to take an in-depth inventory of these underground distractions. Take a day, or a half day, and write down everything that you do. It's really important that you do everything you would normally do; otherwise, you won't get a clear picture of the little things that are holding you back. The big things, the little things, the cups of coffee, the chats with coworkers, the time you spend checking social media. Be ruthless with yourself and totally honest about how much time you're actually spending on Facebook or Instagram. Write it all down for a day. Then commit to eliminating it.

10.

PREDATOR

We are born predators. We have a biological imperative to run fast, to compete, to procreate. We're animals, every last one of us.

It's our true nature, and most of us are running away from this truth as fast as we can.

The word *predator*, like *competition*, has acquired a horrible reputation in the last couple of decades. To be a predator has been redefined as a bad thing, as an immoral thing. But being a predator is essential to our being. For the purposes of this book, I'd like to remind you that being a predator has nothing to do with harming others. It means embracing your physicality. Claiming your magnetism. Making yourself so compelling to look at that people cannot take their eyes off you.

This sort of magnetism is actually a trainable thing. When I was rehearsing my play, my director, Larry Moss, told me he was going to bring in a movement coach, this guy named Jean-Louis Rodrigue.

Now, I'm a former athlete, right? So I said, "I don't need somebody to teach me how to move. Moving is what I do best!"

"Yeah, but it's different on a stage," Larry told me. "There's a freedom of movement you have on an athletic field that doesn't necessarily carry over to other places. So when you're not in that athletic space, you may find that you feel self-conscious or even apologetic about your physical self."

I was skeptical. Then I met Jean-Louis.

Jean-Louis is a professor at UCLA's drama school. He's worked with movie stars, including Leonardo DiCaprio, Margot Robbie, Matt Bomer, Rachel McAdams, and Tobey Maguire, and he really helps his students sink into their physicality. Our goal for *Runt of the Litter* was pretty clear: We didn't want a single audience member to go to the bathroom in the middle of the play, to check their phones, to look at their watches. We didn't want them to take their eyes off the performer.

Jean-Louis has studied predators throughout his career. For *Runt*, we decided what sort of animal he would train me as, and we chose a cheetah. Now, you know we didn't say that explicitly or put it in the program: "Playing the part of the cheetah—Bo Eason." But what happened was nobody looked away from that human on the stage, because (in my case) he had the same characteristics as a cheetah in the wild.

That human being acting as a predator is absolutely mesmerizing. Why? Because he's a little bit untamed. He's just wild enough to keep you aware of his presence and a little unsettled.

Rasmus Ankersen wrote a book called *The Gold Mine Effect*, which is about high performance. One thing in particular stuck with me from that book. Ankersen says that research has found that the brains of domesticated animals are 15–30 percent smaller than those of their wild counterparts. In other words, he says, if you want to thrive in a highly competitive environment (which the wild certainly is), you need to stay a little wild. I love that.

In Tim Grover's book, *Relentless,* he writes, "I guarantee you that everything I know, everything in this book, comes from unlimited access to some of the most excellent and elite performers in the world; I understand how they think, how they learn, how they succeed, and how they fail . . . what drives them to be relentless. It's not all pretty, but it's all true. It's not science. It's raw animal instinct."

These examples make me think about being at the zoo. Let's say you're at the monkey cage, and everyone is having the best time watching the monkeys flip around on their bars and act funny. And then you go to the lion exhibit. I always notice that my heart starts to pound when I get near the lions. Yours, too, probably. You become more serious. You give the lion more respect than you give the monkeys, even though you don't do it consciously.

We're like the monkeys. We don't live behind bars, but most of us live in cubicles and little offices. And we give a wide berth to the predators around us. You want to continue being a monkey—continue being mediocre, being apologetic—fine. But if you want to live like a lion who's escaped the cage, you need to be firing on all cylinders and fully inhabiting your nature. It will affect not just the way you appear to other people but also the way you appear to yourself. You'll give yourself more respect. You'll be bigger and better and stronger.

We are the most dangerous predator on the planet, the most lethal, the smartest, and our lives function better when we acknowledge and embrace that essential aspect of our nature.

I learned several years ago about a tribe of indigenous people who live in the Nuba Mountains of Sudan and exemplify this predator nature. They've been studied because unlike other tribes around them, they are rarely attacked by predatory cats. The researchers pinpointed the difference: This particular tribe walks like predators. They own their bodies and the space around them. They are fully aware of what's going on around them at all times. They know they're not casually strolling through a park, and that knowledge keeps them alive. The predatory cats leave them alone.

The chief of this tribe told the researchers that the only time they get taken down by predatory cats is when they've been drinking.

So put yourself in the mind of one of those cats. You're

just waiting around to jump on someone. And you're watching this particular tribe moving back and forth, back and forth, clearly in tune with everything around them and confident. As the cat, you're going, *Nope, nope, don't want to have that fight on my hands. Not going to attack another predator. That will be too costly to me.* And then one or two of the tribesmen have a few beers and now they're moving with a certain casualness, they're not connecting with the space around them and the ground beneath them like they usually do. The predatory cat sees that, and *bam,* dinner is served.

Most of us aren't in danger of being attacked by wild animals, but if we're not engaged with our predator nature, we're dismissed by the people around us. We're apologizing for who we are. If you look around, you'll notice that's what most people do with their bodies physically. They shrink in on themselves. They apologize with their bodies. Check out the people you see, from the person standing in front of you in line at the coffee place to the weather broadcaster on the TV to the guy texting while he shuffles down the street. Their bodies are screaming, "Sorry! Not trying to invade anyone's space." But great performers—James Brown, Beyoncé, Elvis Presley—are so physically present in their bodies, so confident in the use of their physical space, you just can't look away from them.

Sometimes I ask my clients, "What are the occupations, the people, you can't tear your eyes from?" And they say elite athletes, Navy SEALs, firefighters, even brain surgeons. What's going on there? It's that these people are totally and completely owning their physicality. When you're watching gymnasts flip around on a balance beam, your eyes are glued to them, right? You cannot look away. That's what I want for you—to own your body so thoroughly and so confidently that people's eyes will be glued on you.

Because of how I've been trained, I can literally stand on a stage, perfectly still, for two minutes, five minutes, and hold an audience's attention. I tell them, "Look, we can be here for two hours, because I can do this all day. You're not going to look away, and you're not going to be distracted. And that's because I was trained to be like this. Magnetism is trainable; being in touch with your inner predator is trainable."

That magnetism, that inner predator, changes the way you walk and move your body. Think about elite athletes like Usain Bolt or Simone Biles or Michael Jordan. Eye magnets, every one of them. They move in a certain way. Their eye movements show that they're constantly alert, always taking in what's around them. Even their gait is different from the average person's. Nothing is casual to them. They're exactly like a predator.

Dawn and I were at a bird of prey refuge in Park City, Utah, a few years ago. We saw some of the birds up close when the handlers brought them out. They talked about the birds and then released them to fly.

These birds were just beautiful. We saw a red-tailed hawk, a golden eagle, a falcon, some owls. What struck me most was that they were never distracted. If you're anywhere nearby, that bird knows it. It is never taking its attention off you. And even if it appears to be looking away from you, it knows exactly where you are and what you're doing.

That's how we naturally are. However, the world has taught us to think that our physicality is something to be ashamed of. So we hide our physical nature. We use apologetic body language—some people call them *tells*—to assure the world that we're not going to hurt anyone. Men do this by putting their hands in their pockets. You ever see a guy with his hands in his pockets? It's because he's apologizing for his physicality. Women most often will tend to put their feet really close together or actually cross their feet while they're standing. That cannot be comfortable. And just a side note here: Women are every bit as predatory as men. I'm not talking about masculinity. I'm talking about like how a mama grizzly bear protects her cubs. Or how my mom threw people out of our house when they said we couldn't have our dreams. Or how Dawn is with our kids' dreams and my dreams. Women are just as biologically wired to be predators as men are.

Another tell is when speakers on a stage start doing weird shit with their bodies like shifting their feet or playing with their hair. If you're giving a speech and you've got all these people looking at you, you might start moving your body around in different ways to apologize for your physicality, to let the audience know that you're not violent and you won't hurt them. And I'm telling you that's why people dismiss you.

If you have a dream and a declaration and you're playing your game with your full being, you cannot be dismissed. Your body cannot apologize for that. So I want this implemented everywhere you go. The people I train take this onstage, and they also take it to every room they walk into.

I want to remind you of the only promise that I make to the people I work with one-on-one: If you do what I do, what I tell you to do, people will not have the ability to look away from you.

And then I have my clients actually imagine what that would be like. I want you to do that now. What if people couldn't look away from you? What would that mean to your bottom line in business? What would it mean to your family life? What about your relationship with your spouse? What happens if your kids do not have the ability to look away from you and to dismiss you?

Your entire life will change. That's what will happen.

The Attraction of Danger

Looking for danger is how we have survived for all these centuries. This behavior was encoded into all animals from the beginning of time and remains with us today. We constantly scan for danger. Let's say you're walking down the street in New York City and you're fully embracing your own predatory nature. With every millisecond that passes and without even realizing it, you assess everyone you pass. Not a danger, not a threat, afraid of their own sexuality, dismissed, dismissed, dismissed. You're not consciously doing this. You're just picking them off in your mind and putting them into the "not dangerous" bin. This is how you've survived. It's how you've thrived, whether you're aware of it or not.

Jean-Louis Rodrigue worked with the FBI when they were training operatives to infiltrate Middle Eastern terrorist cells. The FBI sought his expertise because these undercover operatives were being unmasked and then killed at an alarming rate. The reason? Their bodies were betraying them in high-stress situations. These guys took months, sometimes years, to get inside the terror cells. But as soon as they embraced the leader of their cell, the leader could feel that the undercover operative was not who he pretended to be. That's because the leader inhabited his raw animal instincts. He could feel in the operative's embrace his rapidly pounding heart, his anxiety, his nervous sweat. And the leader, the man who fully trusted his instincts, would have the guy killed right there.

Jean-Louis was brought in to train these men to control their bodies, their heartbeat, their respiration, so that their bodies didn't betray them. They more easily infiltrated the terrorist cells, and it saved lives.

You're probably not infiltrating terrorist cells, but your body is undoubtedly betraying you, day after day after day. Your job is to figure out where and when that betrayal happens. Is it when you're onstage giving a presentation? Is it when you're asking for money for your nonprofit? Is it in interactions with your children? Who's going to vote for you, give you their business, give you their respect, if your own body doesn't respect and support you?

As a human, you're tuned in to oncoming danger. You can feel it on the back of your neck. It's how you react to that danger signal that separates predators from prey. But for most of us, those instincts are underused, weak, and flabby. My goal is to bring this predatory nature back for you.

Yes, predators are dangerous. Yes, predators get a bad rap in today's culture. Yes, we're supposed to be pleasant and cooperative at all times. But in the highest expression, predators are noble. They're honest. It's who we are at the core of our being. I'm convinced that if we actually took this on, if we owned our physicality and quit apologizing for our predatory nature and our primal instincts, the world around us would be safer, rather than more dangerous. It's the shame we feel around being who we are that makes us commit crimes, makes us seek out danger, encourages us to harm others so that our physicality can have some expression.

I work with a lot of clients who are retired Special Forces guys. These are some of the most dangerous people on the planet, and I never feel safer than when I'm around them. I feel great. I feel free. I know I'm protected. That's how we feel when we're around people who are unapologetically living fully in their predator self. If you're in a burning building, do you want your firefighters to come in apologetically, or do you want them to be bold and dangerous?

These highly dangerous people make our world safer. It seems counterintuitive, but it's true.

That's why I encourage my clients and am telling you to go counter to the culture. You're being told by the culture that having a lot of confidence is bad. Having big dreams is bad. Being bold and big and sexy is bad, bad, bad. I'm telling you it's the only way to have a shot at being the best in the world at what you do.

Owning your predatory nature is harder than staying small. It's harder than staying safe. But repressing your predatory instinct is difficult, too, and has none of the benefits of embracing your predatory side. It takes a lot of energy to be mediocre. You're constantly pushing down on all your natural expression and creativity. You're walking on eggshells and stepping softly all the time. That's not natural for humans. It's not how we're made. We're made to walk solidly on the ground and to own our connection with the earth. When you put your foot down firmly, you're responsible. You're in charge. You can make things happen.

Here are a few sports analogies: High jumping isn't about jumping high. It's about placing your foot on the ground with as much force as possible. That's what propels you to go higher than anyone else. Similarly, elite runners may look as if they're not even touching the ground, but in fact they are pushing off from the ground with more force than their competitors. Olympic figure skaters propel themselves by digging forcefully into the ice. There is nothing apologetic about how elite athletes move their bodies.

Now, if you've gotten this far in this book, you might think you don't back away or act apologetic. But you do it unconsciously because of years of cultural training. So take steps to reconnect with your predator self. The action steps at the end of this chapter include the daily warm-up I use to reconnect with my predatory nature, and I strongly advise you to use it every day. I promise you it will change your life.

I know that at the time I'm writing this book and you're reading it, we are in a difficult environment to talk about predatory nature. I'm not pretending I don't know that. I totally acknowledge it. Random violence and sexual assault are not what I'm talking about here, though. I'm talking about your true human core. If you bring only half of your physicality, a quarter of your physicality, to go along with your expression of your declaration, you're not going to get very far.

Living as a Predator

So let's talk about how to live as a predator and how to present yourself as a predator without harming other people.

We start by remembering that we already are predators. Our first step is to get in touch with that. When I work with my small groups or my private clients, I take them through my daily warm-up, the Sacred Six. It just knocks the rust off the body that's trying to protect itself. Think of it this way: If you're in one of those occupations we talked about earlier, the ones that basically run toward danger and commitment instead of away from it, you're not trying to protect yourself. You may wear shoulder pads or a helmet or high-tech gear, but you're completely exposed to danger. Your training takes over, and that's what keeps you safe, not your gear.

Most people, however, have built up a suit of armor to protect themselves, not just from the danger around them but from the danger inside of them. The Sacred Six activates your body to throw off that unnatural armor and return to its natural state.

Athletic trainers and coaches use a similar process. When I played in the pros, I was a two-hundred-plus-pound guy going up against guys who outweighed me by a hundred pounds or more. So, as a human being, you look at that sort of situation and you go, *Shit, that is going to hurt. Stay away from those guys.*

But once you go through the ritual of putting on the shoulder pads and applying the eye black and going through the team warm-up to get your body activated, everything changes. At that point, I was actively seeking 350-pound guys to run into. Half an hour before that, I was just a regular guy who happened to be an NFL player, but I hadn't gone through the ritual to put myself in a space where I could fulfill on my job. I wasn't fully inhabiting my body or owning my predatory nature.

This human instrument we've all been given is the most expressive instrument ever created on the face of the earth. Most of us don't treat it with the respect it deserves. We totally misuse it. We make it unhealthy, make it uncommunicative, make it apologize, make it nonthreatening, make it antiseptic and harmless.

That is such a waste of potential.

Take a moment right now and think of the places where you feel your power and where you feel your predatory nature, where you feel as close to your natural self as you can. It might be when you're running, when you're in the gym lifting weights, when you're leading a team at work, when you're playing a musical instrument, when you're singing. Some people find it in church, creative expression, deep meditation, or in fearlessly supporting their family—anywhere they're standing in the basic truth of who they are. Think about lead guitarists of rock bands. Anyone who's gone to a rock concert can tell you just how hot that lead guitarist is. But you take the guitar strap off that person, and they are often not that impressive. The moment that guitar is back in their hands, all eyes are on them. They are owning and expressing their predatory nature through their music, and that is wildly attractive.

The particular place where you feel your most powerful is, at the core of it, rooted in your body. It comes through your body, and it activates your brain. You should live in that space as often as possible. It changes everything.

We've had clients tell us that the Sacred Six ritual changes their lives from top to bottom. They'll say things like, "I completely owned every room I walked into." "I did my warm-up right before a business call, and it was completely different from before." We even had one client tell us, "I had my son do the warm-up with me, and then we went to Costco together and my son noticed that people were just stepping out of our way. They were all looking at us. They even let us go to the front of the line!" We get funny stories like that all the time. The way you carry yourself will change, and your entire life will change along with it. Do the ritual in the morning, before an important meeting or phone call, before getting onstage—any time you need to connect with your predatory nature.

ACTION STEPS

1. Jean-Louis Rodrigue had me watch slow-motion videos of predators running down their prey. Do that. Go online and watch whatever you can find; *National Geographic Wild* on YouTube is a good place to start. You'll get a feel of the freedom of movement, the lack of mistakes, how the predators are totally present to everything around them—the ground, the bushes, the trees, other animals. Watch your pets, if you have any. They're in tune with their bodies and with their environment. That's what you want to be like.

2. The Sacred Six Ritual
Take five minutes or thirty minutes to run through this ritual—it lasts as long as you need it to. Fully expressing yourself in a way that elevates your

performance requires physical preparation, and the Sacred Six is my personal choice for daily preparation.

1. Rock Grounding

A) Take off your shoes and put a smooth stone on the floor. Place one foot on the stone.

B) Lean into the rock and feel its sensation. There may be some discomfort on the sole of your foot. That's the spot you're trying to find. Breathe deeply.

C) After a moment, take your foot off and place it on the floor. Really feel the ground beneath your foot and let the foot open up. Notice the difference in your connection to the ground prior to the stone and after.

D) Go deep. Feel your roots dive a hundred miles into the earth and feel the security of your foot on the ground. The safety and security below you allow the rest of your body to be expressive and perform.

E) Now repeat with the other foot.

2. Mark Your Territory

A) Move around the space and *claim* it.

B) Touch each wall and every other hard surface.

C) Acknowledge each seat, each table, each light, the ceiling, and every inch of the room. You've got this. It's *your* space.

D) Your audience will feel safe and secure with you because this is all your territory and you own it.

3. Warm Up Your Voice

A) Out loud, say, "May may may may may. My my my my my. Mo mo mo mo mo." Repeat it. Move your jaw, stretch your lips, open your mouth.

B) Now, move around the room and repeat the vocal exercise.

4. Send Your Voice

A) Use your body and *throw* your sound across the room. Imagine you're holding a ball in your hand. Throw that ball across the room to the farthest corner—the ball is your voice.

B) As you imagine throwing the ball, say out loud, "One, two, three, four, five." As you pronounce the *v* in *five,* the ball is hitting the corner with your voice. Finish strong on the *v* of the last word.

5. Use Opposition

A) Sense the space behind, around, and above you. As you catapult your words forward ("One, two, three, four, five"), make them reverberate through the entire space.

B) Reach toward one corner of the room with your hand, and use your other hand to reach the opposite corner of the room. While looking at one of those corners, make your voice reach both.

C) Throw the imaginary ball and say, "One, two, three, four, five," making your words travel in opposite directions.

6. Physicalize Your Words

A) Take one or two sentences that you know you'll use in a presentation. How would your body express those sentences? Exaggerate that motion. If you were "brought to your knees," drop to the ground. If you were "hit by a realization," slam your fist into your belly. Give full outrageous physical expression to the words you know you'll speak.

B) Now think of your one true sentence. Take the first word of that sentence and say it like everything you have is riding on it. Use all the power you've got.

That's it! You're ready to face anything now, because you've recruited the full power of your physicality to be present with you throughout your day.

Want to fully express yourself every day as the predator you are? Download my Sacred Six Ritual checklist so it becomes a routine: boeason.com/actionsteps.

11.

NO OBSTACLES, NO HERO

Osaka, Japan—2007. Seventy thousand people are packed into the stands to watch the finals of the men's 100-meter relay, millions more are watching on TV, and the USA team is ready to go. Darvis Patton, Wallace Spearmon, and Tyson Gay tear up the track on the first three legs, while Leroy Dixon is about to take the hand-off from Tyson and bring the race home. Leroy Dixon, who had been a small, skinny, not particularly athletic boy. Leroy Dixon, who had a heart condition as a young child and whose parents were told if he ran, he could die.

Leroy Dixon, who nailed the anchor leg of that race, helped the USA bring home the gold, and ended 2007 as the seventh-fastest man in the world.

Leroy knows something about obstacles. In a talk onstage with Tyson Gay and me in 2017, he said, "I used to get really nervous before races. I'd be walking onto the track with my hoodie pulled up over my head think-ing, *How did I decide to do* this *with my life? What was I thinking?* At Osaka, I thought I was going to fall over at the handoff from Tyson, right there in front of all those people in the stadium, in front of my mom and dad watching on TV. But my body was doing everything. Not me." In other words, all those thousands of hours of practice and drills took over, Leroy's body told his brain to stop worrying, and Leroy was the first one across the finish line.

I've always said that the bigger the obstacle you face, the bigger and better you have to get. Leroy's obstacles, from his early heart condition to his self-doubt before races, were part of who he became as an athlete. He had to push harder, train harder, believe harder, because of the size of his obstacles.

Leroy is a great example of someone who takes charge of his obstacles, instead of letting them define him. Most of us are trained to hope obstacles don't show up. We live our lives hoping for smooth sailing. We pray for things to be easy. In fact, we should ask for obstacles. We should try to create them—bigger obstacles. Gnarlier obstacles. Obstacles that will take everything we've got to overcome them.

Does that seem totally self-defeating? It's anything but. Instead, it's part of how it works when you're aim-ing to become the best. You declare your dream or your goal or your mission and *boom,* you've just created a bunch of obstacles for yourself. These obstacles are your responsibility and your creation because you're the one who made the declaration. I'm not talking about obstacles like Leroy's heart condition—he didn't create that. But by deciding to become a great athlete, he created the obstacle of dealing with that heart condition and overcoming it.

Let's say you declare that you're going to lose twenty-five pounds. Congratulations, you just created a bunch of obstacles for yourself. How will your nutrition change? How will your exercise patterns change? How will your self-talk change? It's not as if those pounds are going to melt off your body overnight just because you asked them to leave. Life doesn't work like that. Here's how it works: When you decide to change, when you lock in on a goal, when you declare a dream, you immediately create obstacles for yourself. The more outrageous the dream, the huger the obstacles.

Think back to me as a nine-year-old in a small town in Northern California. I had no obstacles. I was walking around without a care in the world, right? And then one day, I saw O. J. Simpson on the TV, and I saw my dad's admiring reaction to him, and I said to myself, *I am going to be the person who tackles people like O. J. Simpson.* With that one sentence, I've created obstacles. *You're too small, you're too slow, that's really hard, not many people can do that.* Every rule, everybody's opinion, all kinds of obstacles showed up. So where I could have had a carefree life, instead I created for myself a life full of massive obstacles. I wouldn't trade a minute of it.

Embrace your obstacles. They are what will make you the best.

There's another reason to take on obstacles. Let's say you have a clear path in front of you. There's nothing to slow you down or get in your way. Is that interesting? Will people want to watch that? Will that require you to dig deep and find courage and outperform your expectations? No. That's boring to watch and boring to live. You won't grow at all unless you have challenges to overcome and test yourself against.

Now, a word of warning: I want you to be really honest with yourself about the motivations behind your declaration. Some of your motivations, to be blunt, are BS. They're not from the part of you that's about service or about integrity. They're probably left over from old parts of you that need attention, need to be seen. That's not what this is about.

We all have that need to a certain extent. And sometimes it's necessary because it will get you through the day or through a tough hour. It's that attitude of *Everyone's against me. Forget them. I'm going to do this thing.* That mind-set can motivate you, but it's pretty short-lived and it's exhausting. It's not life-giving. It can be a bear trap if you don't have a deeper motivation.

So here's what I want you to do. Think of yourself as a character that you really admire from literature or from a movie or from real life. What do you love about that person? What do you admire about them? Why are you attracted to them? Do they have unlimited courage? How do they dress? What words come out of their mouth? How do they treat people? At their core, what are they?

And then put yourself in that character and live from there. If you do that, you don't have to expend a lot of energy in this fake, screw-everybody motivation. You can just live into this character that goes hand in hand with your declaration.

Think about that. If your declaration was to be the best quarterback in the world, you can figure out who the best quarterback is right now. What do they do? How do they act? What do they wear? Wardrobe can be really important. I've heard that Robert De Niro will not play a part unless he can find the right hat and shoes for the role. Because you are what you wear. You're telling the audience that you're a particular character when you walk on with a certain hat and pair of shoes. Quarterbacks are exactly the same. They dress a certain way. They look a certain way. They act a certain way. They treat people a certain way. If you want to be like a different position on a football team, everything changes. They dress, they act, they live differently. So what is it for you to live out your declaration? How do you build your character?

Nelson Mandela was incredibly intelligent and astute and massively committed. He was clear about his role in this world. He had a deep sense of faith and humility in his heart. When people have that much faith—I'm not necessarily talking about religious faith here—it's already been worked out. I had faith in my declaration, so it was just a matter of running the miles. No matter what hap-

pens, you keep faith and you keep living out of your declaration. The faith is there. As Florence Scovel Shinn
puts it, "Faith knows it has already received and acts accordingly." Faith sustains you. You've got twenty years
to roam the earth and make this thing happen. People of
faith dress a certain way, talk a certain way, act a certain
way, because they know that, in a sense, the outcome is
already assured. It's done. You just have to get there. And
it's not like it's there one day and not there the next. It's
forever.

I'm not saying things have to be perfect, but take on
the characteristics of this person who has to have ultimate
faith and lead from that inner knowing. This stuff is powerful. Start to be who you want to be today. Come from
a place of clarity and integrity. There is no reason to put
it off.

Obstacles Bring Spiritual Growth

In his groundbreaking book, *The Road Less Traveled:
A New Psychology of Love, Traditional Values, and Spir-
itual Growth*, M. Scott Peck distills the importance of
acknowledging the role obstacles play in our lives. On the
very first page, he writes, "Life is difficult. This is a great
truth, one of the greatest truths. It is a great truth because
once we truly see this truth, we transcend it. Once we
truly know that life is difficult—once we truly understand and accept it—then life is no longer difficult.
Because once it is accepted, the fact that life is difficult
no longer matters."

I love that. Once you accept the fact that life is difficult, that fact no longer matters! You are freed from complaining and whining and wishing things were different.
That acceptance opens up space in your life to just get on
with tackling things and moving ahead. There's no energy wasted after you accept that fact. All your energy,
every ounce of it, can go into forward movement, instead
of being used to keep you stalled and frustrated while you
try to change reality.

Moving beyond your difficulties and growing from
them must be part of your everyday existence. So many
people believe that things should be easier than they actually are. They think that if something is hard, it means
they should quit trying. My kids do this all the time. Let's
say they're working on some specific move that's really
hard, and they just can't nail it. "I suck. I can't do this.
I'm horrible." You know what? None of that is true. They
just haven't practiced enough. What happens if they keep
practicing? Well, they finally master the move, and it's a
huge boost to their confidence. If they quit, it essentially
drives a stake in the ground topped with a big sign that
says, "This is where you quit. You're not good enough to
go past this spot. Nice try, but you're done now."

That's a real dream-killer.

Which would you rather do: Whine and quit, or acknowledge something is hard, tackle it anyway, get on
with conquering it, and then move on to the next obstacle?
I know which route I'd prefer. Since you've read this far,
I think I know which route you'd prefer, as well.

Not everyone gets this. Even after coming to one of my events, sometimes people will make comments about that phrase *the best*. They'll ask, "Well, what about second best?" They're trying to hedge their bets. They're looking for Plan B. But here's the thing. Attempting to be the best is the most humbling thing there is. You have got to resolve any leftover issues you have around getting attention or fame. We do live in a world where fame and notoriety are really important, but I would much rather be the best than be famous. Those two are not the same things. So examine and let go of your need for attention. When you resolve it for real, watch how powerful you become; watch the acknowledgment and attention come. It's a different kind of attention. It's coming because you have your true power and you're attracting a different quality of attention.

Don't fear that it's presumptuous that you're going to be better than everyone else at doing this thing you do. It has nothing to do with other people. It's not about you being better than other people. It's not about dominating other people. It's about dominating the space you're in. It will free you up when you realize you can be the best in the world, but that doesn't mean you have to be the biggest social media star along with it, run the biggest company of your field, or have the longest lines out the door. Your dream is to be the best at what you do and find the best players to be on your team with you. That's it. Stay focused there. Declarations are a class, a way of being, and you can't change that. After you fully commit to it, your declaration takes precedence over everything. It makes the decisions for you. And it is a self-righting mechanism. Remember, your declaration is the thing that rights the ship. It is a living thing, and it takes precedence over everything else. Put it in your head right now. Think of nothing else. You will be building a muscle over time where this sucker speaks for you. It calls every shot. Are you going to this party? Are you going to this movie night out with your friends? Are we going to eat this thing or drink that thing? It's all no or yes based on your declaration. It starts making all your decisions, all your commitments, who you date or marry . . . it calls the shots. It is the filter.

Now, it's mechanical at first, and you're constantly checking in with your declaration, but as the years pass, you'll find you're just living this out automatically and gratefully. Certain things don't go in your mouth; certain things do go in your mouth. You say certain things; you don't say certain things. So if you're, for instance, getting ready for a little gossip session, you just check in with your declaration. Is your declaration about, "Hey, I'm going to be number one at gossip!" or "I'm going to be the most critical person in the world"? That's not a real life; that's just a reaction. People who live like that are living off the scraps of real life. You made your declaration so it could drive your life. Now stand back and let it do what you created it to do.

Welcome the Competition

Anything you do with other people—sports, business, most careers—has a competitive aspect. The obstacles are often built right in. And those obstacles put eyeballs on you, put you at the center of attention. Again, create the biggest obstacles you can. Make your declaration as big as possible. Give yourself something huge to overcome, something worthy to struggle to achieve.

Huge obstacles are so attractive. Imagine a boxing match where one of the boxers is really good and one is really bad. No one is going to watch that fight, because there's not an obstacle standing in the way of the good fighter. But if there are two really good fighters, everybody wants to watch. In fact, you can't look away from it.

So quit trying to get rid of your obstacles. Create more. You want to be in a relationship with your obstacles, to dance with them, to welcome them into your life. They're not bad; they're what you need to have any kind of positive impact in this world.

Remember when we talked about the importance of having a team? Your team shows up because they're attracted to you, to your declaration, to the obstacles that your declaration has brought into being. Why would a team form around you if there wasn't anything to accomplish? If you have an easy declaration, no one will care. It's not going to attract anyone to your side.

Often, I find that my clients need to revisit their declaration about two years after they've made it. They need to upgrade their declaration, or amend it somehow, be-cause it's not big enough. They're not feeling challenged anymore. So if they're not playing a big enough game and then they make a bigger declaration, what happens? That's right. Bigger obstacles. More of a chance to grow. A much higher likelihood that they will become the best in the world at what they do.

Sometimes, upgrading your declaration will mean committing more money to it, and that can cause people to hesitate. Here's the thing about money: You don't have to have money. Money is everywhere. It doesn't have to be your money; you just have to have access to it. Want the convenience of a private jet? You don't have to own a private jet; you just have to have access to a private jet. So once your declaration is up and running, suddenly the money will move in and people with money will start moving in around you. "Hey, who's this person? What's going on with her? You need money? Here you go." That's what millionaires are attracted to. There's this great say-ing, "When artists sit down to dinner, they speak of money, and when bankers sit down to dinner, they speak of art." We need each other. You don't need a how. You need a who. You need the right who, and you'll get them by explaining your what and your why. If you do that in a compelling way, you'll find the who.

So I want you to look forward to upgrading your dec-laration and welcoming the bigger obstacles that come along with that upgrade. For many of us, bigger obsta-cles mean bigger and better competition. What happens when your competition levels up? You have to, as well. When I learned to play tennis, if I played with someone who was as bad as I was, I got worse. When I played with a pro, however, I improved quickly. Tennis is just a stand-in for life here. The bigger your declaration, the bigger your obstacles, the more you can pull out of yourself.

It's the same as playing outside your comfort zone, right? That's why you want your obstacles to be as big as possible; they will keep you outside your comfort zone, and that's the only place improvement lives.

Every good writer knows this. Think about the movies that stay in your mind. A great story has the biggest obstacles: *The Wizard of Oz, Rocky, Braveheart, Gladiator.* But weaker stories—can you even remember those movies? Did they make an impact? Nope. The reason we remember *The Wizard of Oz* is because L. Frank Baum, who wrote the book, put a big scary obstacle in front of Dorothy. That wicked witch and those flying monkeys? We're all still afraid of them! That is great storytelling. It's also a great way to live your life. Make your declaration huge, welcome the big scary obstacles, and acknowledge all the eyes that are on you, watching you fight your way forward.

If you were going to make a movie about climbing Mount Everest, you probably wouldn't start it at the top of the mountain, with the flag being planted and everyone smiling. If the audience doesn't get to see the struggle, they're not going to watch or be engaged. A good storyteller, a good moviemaker, will start at the bottom of the mountain looking up at the snow, at the blizzard that's setting in. It will film the endurance it takes, the life-and-death circumstances, the peril. In other words, the obstacles. Everybody will stay tuned to that movie to see if the climbers make it or not. Audiences want to watch the struggle.

Mount Everest fits in perfectly with our declaration-setting style. You don't just take one giant leap and make it to the peak. You do it in stages and steps. You acclimate. You train. You break it down into smaller and smaller bites and knock those off one by one. That's how you make a goal like climbing Everest attainable.

Think about the movie *Rocky.* How long would you watch that movie if Apollo Creed weren't the heavy-weight champion of the world? He was the biggest obstacle that Sylvester Stallone, as a screenwriter, could come up with. "Let's get this bum fighter. And let's give him the biggest obstacle we could possibly give him so that people will actually follow this bum. We'll put him up against the heavyweight champion of the world and see if he can beat him." What has that just guaranteed the audience? It's guaranteed to deliver heroism, courage, a classic movie. And audiences respond with eyeballs, attention, and ticket money.

You have to do this with your life. Huge declaration, huge obstacles, huge return of attention and support. Think of your life as if it's a movie, and create some crowd-attracting obstacles. Make sure your collar and cuffs match—make sure that whatever comes out of your mouth, you do. In other words, honor your declaration and be true to it. Which, to be honest, is the opposite of what most people do. If you say one thing and do another, your body doesn't know how to process that, and it gets confused. But if you start declaring things and doing them, those goals will come into existence fast. You'll be astonished at how quickly some of your struggles drop away when you match your actions to your mouth.

I want you to respect resistance when you run into it within yourself. Don't try to blow it off. Resistance knows how to take you off your game. It is a worthy opponent, and I have complete respect for worthy opponents. I'm not saying give in to your resistance, but you have to respect the battle it is bringing you. Especially when you're first getting started declaring things. Your resistance will rear its head and go, "Really? Who the hell do you think you are? You're a little too big for your britches," and it will take some nasty swipes at you to test your resolve, to see if you're really up for this.

You're not alone. This happens to everyone. It's a totally normal and appropriate reaction to your making a declaration that you're going to change everything.

I know this is hard. I know it feels like shit. But I just don't care how you feel. Your emotions aren't important. They will mislead you every time you let them.

Edie Allen and Overcoming Obstacles

Edie Allen has a stunning story of self-re-creation. Physically and sexually abused from an early age, she had a baby at fourteen after being repeatedly raped by her mother's boyfriend. Edie ran away from home at fifteen, cycled in and out of foster care, leaned on alcohol and drugs, and then began to pull herself out of that life with the help of nontraditional healing modalities, including Reiki, meditation, intuitive therapy, and every other method that resonated with her soul.

One of those methods was Jon and Missy Butcher's *Lifebook* program. While involved with *Lifebook*, Edie made the conscious decision to put nothing but joyous thoughts into her head. "Ten days into that, I felt like I was on a joy journey. At four in the morning on the tenth day, I woke up hearing this voice saying, 'Get online.' I turned on my computer and saw that a friend had posted a free link to the A-Fest seminar, which is a gathering of change-makers and visionaries, and I was able to watch the speeches for free. That's when I first saw Bo. When I heard him tell his story, I got chills. Not only was he magnanimous; he was magnetic and brilliant and a master of storytelling.

"What I loved most about him was his message to be the best. I really do want to be the best version of myself that I can possibly be, and for so many years I hadn't been living like that. I'd been too focused on survival to focus on a dream of living a better life. But hearing Bo talk made me really want it for myself. He had a three-day live event coming up, but I didn't have money for the tuition or travel to California. All the money I made I reinvested back into my healing."

Edie told a lifelong friend about my seminars, and her friend's reaction was immediate: "Please put together a GoFundMe, and let us send you there." Edie's friends raised the money for her tuition, another friend let her stay at her home in California, and other friends donated airline miles for her flight. She was on her way, not just to my seminar but to a completely different life.

On the first evening of the seminar, I asked everyone to write down ten cool things about themselves. After listening to several people share their ten cool things, I said, "This is all great, but I want to hear that thing that's the hardest to tell somebody." And I called on Edie.

"I'm really scared," she said.

I asked the rest of the audience who else was scared, and every single person put their hand up. "So what cool things do you want us to know about you?" I asked Edie.

"Well, I just got married a month and a half ago, I just got sober two weeks ago, and when I was fourteen I got pregnant by my mother's boyfriend . . ." Edie went on, finishing with, "I have spent the rest of my life trying to heal and to help as many people as I can to heal from their traumas and to live into their dreams. I've worked as a massage therapist for the last twenty years, and now I'm a life coach."

"Wow. You just set the bar for the weekend," I said.

After the seminar was over, Edie had dinner with a friend who knows Steven Tyler, the lead singer of Aerosmith. Tyler had started a nonprofit called Janie's Fund to help girls who've been neglected and abused. "Would you please tell Steven Tyler I said thank you for the work he's doing?" she asked her friend. "Why don't you tell him yourself?" her friend responded. He texted Tyler, who texted back that he would call Edie the next day.

"I'm like, *Sure he will,* but he did. And because we've both been in recovery, we had that common language. Because of Bo, I was able to talk to Steven Tyler as a colleague, not as someone who was above me. He invited me to come to a fund-raiser for Janie's Fund and flew me and my husband to Los Angeles. They raised over $2 million that night, and I got to be part of it. And he asked me to speak at next year's gala."

Edie says her dream now is to write a book and help as many people as she can with her story, to get on as many stages as possible, and to continue her transformational healing work with as many people as she can reach. She's been a speaker with an empowerment series for Lululemon and other organizations and has been added to the speaker's bureau for RAINN (Rape, Abuse & Incest National Network) started by Tori Amos.

"One of the biggest things I learned from Bo was that how successful I become depends on how much or how well I show up. I simply couldn't show up before. I was invisible. I was just trying to survive. Now, I want to be the bravest storyteller alive."

Edie spoke about how to keep her mind-set strong throughout the challenges of becoming the best. "When I find myself slipping into lazy thinking or negative self-talk, I use what I call my *reach* process. I deliberately *reach* for a thought that feels better than the one I'm having. And then I *reach* again for one that feels even better. I keep reaching until I feel the best that I can possibly feel.

"Sometimes I stop and *reach* for something beautiful. There is beauty all around us, and reaching for something beautiful to focus on reminds me to be my most beautiful self, inside and out. Feeling beautiful is part of me being my best self.

"One day, I was picking up a prescription for my seventy-six-year-old godmother, Patsy. Her drugstore was in a questionable part of town with lots of interesting characters hanging outside the door and the smell of urine strong on the pavement. Walking in, I found myself having thoughts that weren't so pleasant. So I decided to reach for something beautiful in this not-so-beautiful environment, and just as I did, I saw, painted high on the wall in black letters at least five feet tall, the word *beautiful*. I smiled knowing that I am never alone in my efforts to be my best and beautiful self."

Get the World on Your Side

Most goal-setting coaches say things like, "Make your goals realistic."

Why? Why would you do that? That's just stupid. Make them impossible. If you make your goals impossible, you know what happens? Everyone shows up to support you. John F. Kennedy told the whole world that we were going to put a man on the moon and bring him home safely, and we did. He basically threw it out there because we were behind the Russians in the space race. He created this huge obstacle: Let's get a man on the moon. And this country made that happen, even though JFK died before it took place. Think about that. The man who made the declaration died. Yet the declaration lived on. It was successful.

Most people don't play that big. They don't participate. So they don't face loss, but they don't get to feel the triumph of victory, either. And they don't attract a team to help them fulfill their declaration.

Never underestimate the attractiveness of a big, seemingly impossible goal. I am constantly amazed at the people who have stepped up and asked to be part of Axel's supposedly impossible declaration of playing in both the NFL and the NBA. People show up who are the best at what they do, whether it's speed work, nutrition, sports medicine, or sports psychology. They want to work with him because they are attracted to this gigantic dream. And so they offer their help to make it happen.

I gave a speech recently, and afterward, a woman in the audience came up to me and introduced herself. Catherine Garceau was a silver medalist in synchronized swimming, and now she works with athletes using a modality called *tapping*, which helps clear issues in the brain and body. She told me, "I heard about your son's dream, and I'd like to help him." They're still working together to this day.

Another person who's shown up is Dr. Ara Suppiah, who's been the doctor of the Ryder Cup team and the

Olympic golf team. He heard Axel's story and jumped right in. He contacted me and said, "I'd like to help him. What's he eating? Can I come to California and take his blood? I want to see if he's allergic to anything and figure out what he should and shouldn't eat and supplement him in the places where he's weak." So he did all that, and he became part of Axel's story, too.

The same thing happened with Leroy Dixon—one of the world's fastest men, remember? I was talking with Leroy about Axel and said, "Look, if he's going to be the best athlete on this planet in twelve or twenty or forty years, he's going to need to be the fastest as part of that. Can you help him?"

Leroy said, "Heck, yeah!" And he's been working with Axel ever since. In fact, a little while back, when none of us could get Axel to one of his workouts, Leroy said, "I'll pick him up and bring him back home. I don't want him to miss his workout." This is an Olympic sprinter stepping up to help an eleven-year-old kid. This is the attractive power of an impossible dream. I was just bowled over.

That's the power of a huge dream. That's the sort of attraction that a huge declaration can have. The world comes to your aid, because the bigger your declaration, the bigger your obstacle. Everyone loves a dream. When the right people see someone with a huge dream, they want to be part of it. They actually get fulfilled in their own dreams when they're inside of yours, when they're helping you achieve your dream.

Don't hold back. The harder you push yourself, the greater the reward you'll find.

ACTION STEPS

1. Look back at the declaration you wrote earlier. Is it challenging enough? Does it create enough obstacles? Will it force you to grow as much as possible? If you can make your declaration bigger, do it. Rewrite it and recommit to it. A bigger declaration will by necessity create an even better you, because you'll be playing up to a higher level. In addition, a bigger declaration will attract a higher quality of excitement and dedication from the people who show up for you. Every time you make your dream and your obstacles bigger, you change everything around you, including the people who are attracted to your dream.

2. Name your favorite character of all time. This could be a literary character, someone from a movie, someone from a TV show—we all have a character who really speaks to us. Mine is General George Patton. Figure out who yours is, and then ask yourself why. Write down why you picked that person. What do they represent to you? If you're like most of my clients, you chose someone who had major obstacles to overcome. You're attracted to their courage. You probably don't want to live

out their exact challenges in your life, but this exercise can show you what you're attracted to. List the obstacles they had to overcome and list your own obstacles. You'll undoubtedly find some overlap there.

3. Name your five favorite movies of all time (or books, if you're not a movie person). Now find the common theme in those movies that matches the theme of your life. Sometimes you have to do a little wrestling to find the theme, but I guarantee you it's there. For instance, my list includes *Raging Bull* and *Billy Elliot*. How the heck do those two fit together? Well, what are their obstacles? They're both guy characters who are basically warriors and excel at something. They're both looking for where they fit in and can bring that excellence. And neither one of them has a place for their excellence—kind of like a warrior without a war. That's one of the themes of my life; I'm always trying to find a platform to put all of this TNT I feel inside my body. I can't run my head into people at twenty-five miles an hour anymore, so I have to keep finding new ways to channel that sort of energy and drive.

4. I want you to write out your Plan B, your fallback plan, the thing you'll do if this doesn't work

out. Now burn it. I don't believe in Plan B, and neither should you.

5. Make a point of remembering every single day that you are the creator of your own obstacles, and I don't mean that in a negative sense. You are the one stating your dreams. Once you state your dreams, you've created a set of obstacles you have to overcome to get to the finish line. Ask yourself every day if your dream is big enough, if your obstacles are hard enough. And if they aren't, make them bigger. Welcome the challenge. Welcome the push to live outside your comfort zone. You're the best, goddammit.

12.

RULES TO LIVE BY

've given you a lot to absorb in this book. The action steps will help you put your plan into motion, so give them your care and attention and respect. They're like a road map you can follow on the way to fulfilling your declaration.

This chapter gives you the road signs, if you will, to use along the way. These are the rules that you need to incorporate into your life every day, every minute, to ensure your success.

Do every single one of these, live your declaration with joy and faith and love for yourself and everyone around you, and you'll be the best.

Rule #1: I Know There's No Plan B for My A-Game

Isn't it great to be alive right now? We have more options and choices than ever before in the history of humankind. That makes for a much better, more fulfilling life, right?

Well, maybe. I think we have too many options right now. If something doesn't work out, there's always another thing you can fall back on. Being married is harder than you thought? Hey, divorce is no big deal, and there are a ton of single people out there just waiting to meet you. Tired of the demands of your job? Find something easier. Life's too short to work hard. Having a hard time deciding between a healthy meal and the gooey, greasy, yummy-looking pile of fried stuff your friends are diving into? Oh, go ahead. You can eat better tomorrow.

I say this over and over again: When you make a declaration, you cut off your options and simplify your life immensely. Think about it. Let's say you decide to do a sixty-six-day theme where you give up sugar. Now, you might start out whining and complaining because you have to read labels at the grocery store and ask in restaurants, and it limits what you can eat, plus you *like* sugar. But once you get past the initial stage of finding out all the crazy places sugar hides (goodbye, ketchup and mayonnaise), you'll discover a true sense of freedom. All the arguments about eating healthy you've had with yourself in the past will just drop away. You walk through the grocery store and you might look at the candy section or the baked goods or the crackers or even the deli dishes, but you don't have to argue yourself out of buying them. You don't even have to make the decision there in the grocery store because you've already made your decision not to eat that junk.

Go ahead, simplify your life. You'll be amazed at the energy and brain space you have left over when you're not fighting with yourself over something like whether or not you're going to eat some junk food.

Rule #2: I Will Be Unreasonable

I've talked about this before, but the odds against most really big dreams are just staggeringly high. You want to play in the NFL? There's 0.03 percent chance you're going to make it. The chances for Axel to reach his dream of playing in the NFL and the NBA are 0.0009 percent—statistically impossible, for the most part. And I love that. When people see those kinds of odds and they lick their chops and say, "Let's go!" like I do, that's what I like to see. Most people see those odds and say, "Oh, shit, I'll never do it." That's not what I'm teaching you here. Dream big; dream huge; be totally unreasonable with your dreams. Lauren Holiday, the first National Women's Soccer League player to have her jersey retired when she stopped playing, has been unreasonable all her life. She had open-heart surgery at the age of three and refused to stay quiet during the recovery process. She was playing tackle football with her brother not long after her surgery (without her parents' knowledge, of course). Lauren had a drive and a dream to be active, and nothing was going to stand in her way.

Remember that your dreams can and should get bigger. Your declaration should grow. That's all part of being unreasonable—you change and your dreams change and the obstacles you create for yourself get bigger and more difficult. We're surrounded by people who are fine with mediocrity, who don't want anything other than comfort and safety. And yet here we are, running full tilt at completely unreasonable odds, climbing over obstacles that would make most people say, "Eh, too hard," and reach for a beer and the remote. Be unreasonable. That's where the rewards are.

Rule #3: I Know There's Only One Way Out—Quit

Once you make your declaration, there's really only one way out of it, and that's to quit. You have to fully, consciously, totally quit. Otherwise, this thing is going to happen.

You can quit for an hour, and I have done that. My kids do that, too. They start crying. They're like, "I can't do it. Oh, I quit." They lie on the sofa with their head down, and they quit. And I get a huge smile on my face when they do that, because I know what's about to happen. I know they're going to lie there and cry and mope for about an hour, and then they're going to get up and reengage. Because even as young as they are, they know that if they keep lying there, if they lie there month after month, year after year, their life will be filled with regret.

I'm not promising you that your life will be filled with happiness or joy or unicorns or whatever. But it *will* be filled with greatness and inspiration.

So whatever it is you're doing, whether it's figuring out how to write a book or be a parent or thrive in a marriage or bring a business into existence, and you know there's no quitting, when you surrender to it and recognize that you're fully in it, that's when things start to happen. Other people will drop by the wayside. Other people will quit. People who are better than you will quit. Guys who were way better athletes than I was in high school quit, and that made room for me and my dream. They quit, and I passed them up. I didn't beat them. They beat themselves.

This is always the case. If you look at pro sports, it's rarely the ones who are the most talented who are at the very top of the league. They're not better than a thousand other athletes. They're just more hardheaded. They don't have that quitter molecule in their body.

Be like them.

Rule #4: I Will Only Work with the Best

A lot of people are intimidated about seeking out the top people in their field. They think they're not available, or they tell themselves, "Why would the best person at this want to spend time with me? They're too busy."

Here's why that's wrong thinking: If you work with someone who's mediocre or even second best, you'll learn how to be mediocre or second best. Because not only do they not know how to coach you to be the best; they don't know how to be the best themselves. If they did; they'd be at the top instead of somewhere back in the pack.

That's not what this book is about. That's not what your life is about.

The second best are always nervous. They don't trust themselves, and if you approach them for advice or coaching, they'll think you're going to pass them up, and that makes them afraid. And let's face it: You are going to pass them up, because you have more commitment than they do. So not only can't they help you; they won't help you because they're too busy clinging on to their place.

But the top coach wants you to pass them. They like it when you show up because they need the competition. I love it when I see a speaker who really challenges me, because it means I have to up my game. I actually want to thank them for being so damn good because it makes me better.

That's why I love the fights of the 1970s with Muhammad Ali and Joe Frazier, with Roberto Durán and Sugar Ray Leonard. They had these unbelievable fights where it just looked like they wanted to kill each other. I had a picture taken with Durán and Leonard, and even though they were both half my size, I was nervous because I thought they might kick each other's ass right there. Turns out they were actually friends. They respected and honored and loved each other because of what they brought

out in each other. They made each other better. That's
what the best do for their top competitors, and that's what
the top person in your field is going to do for you. You
just have to show up and ask.

Rule #5: I Won't Go It Alone

We're social creatures. It's just the way we're made. We
create community; we live in groups; we want connection.

So in some ways, the declaration and the drive to be
at the top, to be the best, might seem to fight with that
need for connection. I do get pushback on this fairly often. "Well, Bo, for me to be the best, that's pretty selfish.
That's not really serving the world."

My response always is, "You sure about that? In my experience, it's more than serving the world. It's serving
everyone around you either to play at your level so they can
go right to the top with you or to eliminate themselves."

Every time I commit to being the best, I drag a group
of people with me. Some of them don't even know they're
coming along. They get caught up in the declaration, in
the tidal wave of the declaration, and they ride that wave,
which is totally cool.

I'm really interested in what will happen to the guys
who are close to Axel. They're going to get caught up in
what he's doing, and their parents are going to get caught
up in it. And I can guarantee you that for some of them,
their reaction will be, "Well, Axel is going to do it, and
his parents don't seem to have any doubts that he's going
to do it, so let's do it, too."

It's just like when Roger Bannister broke the four-minute mile barrier. Bannister ran a mile in 3:59:40 in May 1954, and at another race in June—less than two months later—he and John Landy *both* ran the mile in under four minutes. Ten years after that, a high school kid, Jim Ryun, ran the mile in under four minutes. In the years since Bannister first broke the record, more than 1,400 male runners have broken the four-minute barrier. He showed them that it was possible. Once people see something is possible, they adjust their dreams and go for it. Instead of thinking, *This is impossible. Why am I even trying?* it spurs their effort to a higher level.

When you perform at your very best, it actually frees other people up to commit to their dreams. You bring them along with you. You spend some of your energy on them and set an example of true commitment to a worthy declaration. People will rise up with you. You're truly never doing this alone.

Rule #6: I Will Live Beyond My Current Capacity

You're on this journey to being the best, and you know by now that there is no such thing as comfort along this path. You need to employ deliberate practice. A lot of what you do will be a struggle. You need to learn to think of your success in terms of being a biological necessity.

Our entire society is training for ease and luxury. All around us people are focused on comfort and risk aversion. That's not us. We are training for adversity. We are training to live beyond our capacity. And that's why we're going to succeed—we are constantly forced to adapt and to challenge ourselves.

I want you to constantly keep in mind that Navy SEAL mantra: "If it doesn't suck, we don't do it." When your brain tells you you're done, you're not. When your brain is screaming, *I'm done!* you are actually only at about 40 percent capacity. Think about that next time you want to quit.

Rule #7: I Will Not Allow Wimpy-Ass Timelines

You are in this for the long haul. As Anders Ericsson says, "There are no shortcuts, and there are no prodigies."

Nobody great has ever just shown up and been great without a ton of hard work. In this world that's promising you hacks and shortcuts and telling you there's not enough time to be the best, you'll be tempted to shorten your timelines. Don't do it.

When you make your declaration a twenty-year commitment, you also schedule in championships all along the way. You monitor your progress and see where you need to increase your effort. And you stay the course.

That long-term commitment is what gives you power.

Rule #8: I Will Stay Wild

The brains of domesticated cats are 30 percent smaller than the brains of their wild counterparts—30 percent. Think about that. Ask yourself what you can do to stay wild. What can you do to tap into your animal instincts?

If you want to fulfill your declaration, you need access to your wild side.

A lot of us work in cubicles or office spaces or glass boxes. We do the same thing day after day. We're cut off from our wildness and our primitiveness. Our ability to adjust to a changing environment or different circumstance has been whittled away over the years. That's what you want to get back: your wildness, your competitive spirit, your ability to tap into your animal nature.

Rule #9: I'm a Player, Not a Fan

Players compete. They don't sit on the sidelines, drink beer, throw popcorn, and yell insults at the actual players. Fans, however, don't know victory, and they don't know defeat because they don't get off their asses and get into the game.

If you're really dedicated to your declaration, you protect it with everything you have, just like lions protect the prides they're in and grizzly bears protect their cubs. This means you let your instincts take over sometimes and do what has to be done to guard and protect your dream and the mentality you've built. You leave nothing on the field when you're a player. You put it all out there, every time.

Rule #10: I Won't Let the Ball Touch the Ground

This is the standard you want to play up to. In truth, the ball will touch the ground, especially in the beginning. But there will come a time where it doesn't, because that's the commitment.

Most of us are walking around with zero standards because we don't know we're supposed to have any. That gives you too many options. And as you know, I like fewer options.

It sounds crazy, but I guarantee you that one strategy, that one rule, is what's made me successful in everything I've ever done, including being a husband and a father. You know those balls are going to be thrown. You know the standard at which you're going to take care and respect that ball. Substitute *marriage* or *parent* or *friend* or *professional* or anything for *ball* and that's how I'm showing up. That ball ain't touching the ground. That's the commitment I bring, and that's the commitment I want you to bring.

Rule #11: I Will Be the First One on the Field and the Last One Off

This rule pretty much speaks for itself. Think Jerry Rice, all-time touchdown leader for the NFL, and how he held himself to this standard for practice. You'll see this principle in action in the next chapter. Think of the CEOs who are the first ones there in the morning and the last ones there at night. Think about Stephen King, who writes two thousand words every morning. How about Joyce Carol Oates, who writes from 8:30 a.m. to 1:00 p.m. every day, unless she's traveling. On the road, she writes from 10:00 p.m. to 3:00 a.m.!

Find that commitment inside yourself and bring it to your life.

Rule #12: I Will Keep a Generous Spirit

No one exemplifies this better than Jerry Rice. The way he practiced changed the way I saw the rest of my life. His full-speed running to the end zone on every passing drill opened my eyes. He set the standard, and at the time for me, it was just for football, but it impacted every part of my life after that. It changed how I approached marriage. It changed how I approached parenting. It changed how much I was willing to give of myself onstage. I really had to look at myself and go, *Wow, I bet I can give more. There might be more spirit in me and more generosity in me than I'm giving, and I thought I was maxed out.*

Rule #13: I Will Live in the World of My Dreams, Not My Distractions

Your dream, your declaration, takes precedence over everything else. Whenever you are faced with a distraction, opt for the dream. Want to play some goofy game on your phone or lose time on some social media? Sure, go ahead. Or opt for your dream. This is hugely empowering. You'll get to a point where you realize, *I don't live in this world of distraction. I live in the world of my dream. I'm not distracted from my journey.*

Rule #14: I Will Be a Champion at Recovery

When we were preparing to produce *Runt* in New York City, my coach whipped me into top physical shape. We were trying to transform my body into looking like a football player again. I'll never forget when he said to me, "What do you think is the most important thing we've got to do in the next eight weeks?" I was thinking nutrition, lifting weights, getting in better shape, right? And he said, "No, sleep. Sleep is the number-one thing." I couldn't believe it.

He was right, of course. If you look at the best player in the NFL (Tom Brady) and the best player in the NBA (LeBron James), they are among the oldest, but they are the best at recovering. They've made it part of their training. This holds true in other disciplines; in *Peak,* Ericsson says that the very top piano players sleep more than other piano players. Five hours a week more sleep is the thing that distinguishes them. So guard your recovery time and make it part of your life.

Rule #15: I Will Never Move a Piano

Moving pianos is not part of my job. Unless your declaration is to be the best piano mover in the world, it shouldn't be part of yours, either. You're here to do the things you do best and the things that consistently move you toward becoming the best.

Remember, you're never maintaining. You're either advancing or retreating. You're either gaining ground or losing ground. And if you find yourself moving a piano, you are retreating from your declaration.

Rule #16: I Will Get a Dawn

To stay focused on your declaration, you need a team, and that team needs a leader. For me, as you know, that person is Dawn. She is here to help me course-correct so I can mow down the obstacles and set up the opportunities. Your life will function immeasurably more smoothly when you find the person who handles things for you.

ACTION STEP

If you haven't yet committed to a sixty-six-day challenge, do it now. I want you to pick the thing you're most hesitant to do, whether it's eliminating TV or training for a race or writing every morning for fifteen minutes or quitting sugar or whatever it is that makes you quake in fear, and do that thing.

13.

YOUR STORY MATTERS

Story is everything.

Can you live out your declaration without knowing your own story? I say you can't. I say you have to understand your personal story on the most intimate level to reach your dream. I'm not saying you need to sit down and write out a one-person play like I did. We're not all writers. But you have to know what story you're telling *yourself* about yourself, because that greatly influences the story you tell the *world* about yourself, and it determines the life you will live.

If you tell yourself you're twenty pounds overweight and a loser, that's the story you're going to live out. Is that really your story? Or do you want to change it and change the course of your life?

When you truly and fully live into your story, you don't have to tell people what that story is. I never have to say, "Hey, I'm Bo. I'm a really hard worker, I'm super-disciplined, I'm faithful to my wife, I love my kids, and I'm here to help other people achieve their dreams." Your character is revealed through the story of who you are and how you act in the world. When your story is at a high level, it demands that listeners play up to that level. It also promises them the sort of future they'll have if they hang out with you.

That's why we need such long-ass timelines. You really do require twenty years to fully live into your declaration. You're going to be off course; you're going to stumble; you're going to throw yourself on the floor and shout, "This is too hard. I quit!" Twenty years is long enough to deal with the inevitable hiccups and bumps along the way, and it's also long enough that you'll experience noticeable victories and positive changes.

When I was nine years old and my dad was hollering about O. J. Simpson being the most amazing, beautiful athlete he'd ever seen, I knew it would take me twenty years to turn myself into the sort of athlete who could tackle a guy like O. J. Simpson. How do you stop the most beautiful runner in the sport? Who do you have to become? I was determined to find out, and along the way, I figured I'd get my dad's love and respect, too. I knew my dad loved me—"You're the best in there, goddammit," was a pretty inspirational way to start every day—but I wanted to show him that I believed it, too. Show him that I could pay back his belief in me by being the best in the world at stopping the fastest football players.

I was really young when my story came to me. For most people, it happens later—sometimes even into your sixties or seventies—before you're hit by lightning and realize what it is you could be best in the world at. We all have our own story. We all have our own declaration to live into. Make sure you tell yourself the right story and live out the right story. Find the story that empowers you, not the story that has you victimized and fueled with self-hate.

Decades after I first saw O. J. Simpson on the TV and wrote out my twenty-year plan to be the best safety in the NFL, years after O. J. was on trial for the murder of his ex-wife Nicole, months after we had produced *Runt of the Litter* in New York City, Dawn's phone rang one day, and the voice on the other end said, "Hey. Is Bo there? This is the Juice." Dawn's face turned white, and she handed me the phone.

"Hey, Bo, this is the Juice. Some friends of mine saw your play. I hear it's a great play and that I'm like a pivotal part in it, and I just really appreciate that you didn't take any cheap shots at me. I know that would have been really easy to do," O. J. Simpson said to me.

I have no idea what I said to him. Here's this guy I had looked up to my whole life, and then that whole mess went down. I was still in awe of him and also a little bit afraid. He had basically started my first twenty-year plan, and I really had no idea how to react to him. I mean, he marked a moment that defines me, that defines my story, that defines my whole life. I might never have become who I am if not for O. J. Simpson.

That first O.J.–inspired plan led to the second plan and the third plan. At its heart, each plan is a story about who I wanted to become.

I told myself the story first. The story, the belief, came first. The plan—the how-to—came later.

That's what you need to do. Find your story. Tell it to yourself in the best way you can—through words, through pictures, through action.

I Haven't Always Been like This

People come to these events we put on, and I stand there onstage and tell them things, and they just assume that it's always been like this for me and that I'm ahead of them somehow. Bo Eason, NFL player. Bo Eason, playwright and actor. Bo Eason, successful motivational speaker.

They don't know what was going on behind the scenes, how Dawn and I had to draw on what I call that generosity of spirit, that belief in the story, to keep going.

So I tell them the story of what it was really like. We were totally broke, I was working as a delivery guy, delivering food to celebrities at five o'clock in the morning—some of whom were our friends and they had no idea we were doing this to make money—and we were trying to get the play produced.

One of the catering company's clients was a very famous producer in Beverly Hills. Every morning, I'd drop his breakfast, lunch, and dinner on his porch at five in the morning and keep going. After we delivered the food, we'd start working on the play, and at night, we'd put the play up in front of anybody who would watch. One night after six months of this, that very producer walked up to me after the play and said, "I want this to be my next movie." I looked at him and thought, *If you only knew that I delivered your food to you this morning.*

So that's what this generosity of spirit will bring you— you're inspired to stick with it because you never know where it will lead, but you absolutely have to give it your full heart, your full attention, because it's your story and it's your life.

Sometimes people think we just tried this story thing, it worked out for us, we got lucky, we didn't have to fight any critics or go through any hard times—well, that's not the case. It's been a struggle and a fight, and sometimes it's heartbreaking, and it's been worth it every step of the way. That's what I want you to understand. If you stay faithful to your story, if you hold on to that generosity of spirit, you will never regret it.

It's hard for all of us. Dawn and I weren't always successful. No one is always successful. That's why the twenty-year plan is so vital. Without that plan, it's really easy to quit. It's just so easy to go on to the next shiny object. You separate yourself from the culture once you decide to stay loyal to your story, and that loyalty can feel hard sometimes and socially isolating more often than not. Many people will just bail on themselves as soon as the first hiccup comes along. In fact, they'll bail before the first hiccup comes along. Or they see future pain on the horizon, and they don't even start because of the future pain. I promise you, if you commit to this twenty-year plan, the first hiccup will come, for sure, and then you'll blink and it will be over. But your next hiccup is right behind it. And you have to stay committed through that one, and all the others, as well.

Remember, by declaring your plan, you've caused obstacles to arise. You've created conflict. You've created tension. That's what makes a good story. That's what makes an interesting life. If you embody that story into your molecules, internalize it, and make it part of your everyday life, you can tell your story without even saying a word. People will follow you just because of how you move through the world. Your story is physically moving through time in the real world, embodied by you. I cannot begin to tell you how attractive people find that. They want to be part of that because they can tell it's a great story.

You're writing your own story. You're the author of this thing. Would you write about someone who just gave up? Would you write about someone who blamed everything and everyone around them? Or would you rather write about someone who lived through great obstacles and changed everything along the way? Which story do you think is more life-giving? Which story will attract other people? Which story lets you choose yourself, instead of waiting for someone else—an employer, a producer, a partner—to choose you?

Choose yourself. Take your life into your own hands

and write the story you want to read when you're done living.

And remember, I care about what you desire. I care about what you're committed to. I care about what you've declared and how to help you see that fulfilled in your life.

Start living that life today.

Let me close this book with a story I like to tell about Jerry Rice. Jerry Rice was the greatest football player ever to play the game, and the guy in second place is so far behind it's not even close.

I used to play against Jerry Rice. It was a *nightmare* to play against this dude. But toward the end of my career, I got traded to the San Francisco 49ers. And now the greatest player in the history of the game and I were on the same team. And I said, "Good. I want to see what he's made of. I want to see what he does."

Up until this point, I had always been the first person on the field at practice and the last person to leave the field. I'd made that contract with myself when I was a kid, and I'd kept that contract. No one ever beat me.

Then I met Jerry Rice.

On the first day of training camp with the 49ers, it was like 110 degrees. Unbelievably hot. An hour and a half before practice started, I was in the locker room getting dressed. No one else was in there. Joe Montana was not in there. Ronnie Lott was not in there. Randy Cross wasn't in there yet. Just me. And I thought, *I'm beating them all again, and I'm going to keep this roll going. No one is going to beat me.*

So I walked out into that heat, and I looked around at the practice field. *Good, I'm the first one here.* Then I looked over. And guess who was right there? Jerry Rice. The greatest player in the history of the game.

By now, it probably makes total sense to you, but to most people it won't. They're thinking he should have just been chilling somewhere. He had nothing to prove, right? He was already the best in the world at what he did. But he was out there on the field. I was like, *Damn. No one's ever beaten me onto the field before.* So I was a little pissed.

An hour and a half later, the rest of the team came out for warm-ups, and the passing warm-up was sixteen guys in a line, all receivers. Jerry Rice was in this line along with everyone else battling to make the team. Joe Montana and Steve Young were there to throw some balls to these receivers, just easy, to warm everybody up.

First guy in the line went up. Joe snapped the ball. The receiver took off at half speed, broke off on a little slant. Joe threw the ball. The receiver caught it and stopped. He tossed the ball back to Joe and got back in line. Next guy went up. Same thing. All-pro guy, cool, broke off on a little slant. Joe threw the ball. The receiver caught the ball. Stopped. Walked the ball back to Joe. Handed Joe the ball. Back in line.

And then Jerry Rice went up. This is what he did: Full speed. *Bam.* Broke off on a slant. Caught the ball. Gone. One hundred yards. We're like, *Damn. Where the hell is he going?* A hundred yards into the end zone. Turned around, full speed, all the way back. Handed the ball to Joe. Back in line.

The next guy went up. He was going to run a little out pattern. All-pro guy, cool, broke off a little out. Caught the ball. Stopped. Walked the ball back to Joe. Handed Joe the ball. Back in line.

Jerry Rice went up again. Full speed. Broke it off. Caught the ball. Gone. Gone, one hundred yards over and over and over again for three hours. He must have run ten miles of those sprints. I'd never seen anything like it. I went up to him after practice, after the three hours were done, and said, "Jerry, hey, man, damn. What in the hell are you doing? The running—why do you do that?"

And Jerry Rice said, "Bo, that's very simple. I do that because every time these hands touch a ball, this body ends up in an end zone somewhere."

Now, that's a great story. That's the story Jerry Rice told himself, and that story made him the greatest football player ever. That day changed my life forever. You know those sixteen guys running drills? They were my teammates, too, and I can't remember most of their names. But Jerry Rice—we all know Jerry Rice. We know his name because of the story he told and the way he lived out that story on the football field.

Several years ago, I was conducting a wedding for some friends—yeah, I'm a certified preacher man in the state of California—and I started my sermon off with, "Whenever I think of marriage, I think of Jerry Rice." And all the guys are like, *"Hell, yeah! Jerry Rice!"*

Here's what I said next: Jerry Rice changed how I think about life. His generosity of spirit changed everything I do. He was willing to give everything he had, all the time. What would your life look like if you turned up in that way? What could your life be if you lived out that story in all your relationships, starting with your relationship with yourself? How profound would the changes be if you brought the spirit of Jerry Rice to your marriage, your parenting, your friendships, your business?

That's what I want you to take away from this book. Be like Jerry Rice. Give everything you have, every time. Tell yourself that story and live by it.

I guarantee that when you look back over a life lived that way, you'll realize that you were the best, goddammit. I can't imagine living any other way.

ACTION STEP

Remember the story you wrote for the action step in chapter 1? I want you to get it out and look at it. Figure out if you're telling yourself stories you want to live by or if you're living out stories that are not yours—ones that were passed down to you by your family or your culture or your religion, ones that don't enrich your life and allow you to grow into your declaration.

Now, write your best life story—the one you want to live.

For tips and insights into how to refine your story, go to boeason.com/actionsteps. You'll also discover other stories to help inspire you.

Bo Eason Action Step CTAs

CHAPTER	EXERCISE	BLURB IN BOOK	MINI-COURSE WOULD HAVE
1	Write who you are/where you see your life heading.	For more questions to ask yourself about who you are and where you're headed in the future, check out boeason.com/actionsteps.	More questions to solicit where you are/where you are headed Worksheet
3	Declaration (name it, draw it, write a letter).	Go to boeason.com/actionsteps for your Declaration Worksheet and examples of powerful letters and declarations.	Examples of letters Preparation Exercise
4	Eliminate distractions' "Never Do Again" list	To truly make your distractions a thing of the past, fill out your Preparation Exercise at boeason.com/actionsteps. You'll also find what's next with your "Never Do Again" list.	"Never Do Again" Part 2 (this can be from chapter 5!)
7	Schedule a championship	Download your free calendar to schedule your championship and plan your 66-day challenge at boeason.com/actionsteps.	Calendar :)
10	Predator/Sacred Six	Want to fully express yourself every day as the predator you are? Download my Sacred Six Ritual checklist so it becomes a committed routine: boeason.com/actionsteps.	Sacred Six checklist
13	Write your best life story.	For tips and insights into how to refine your story, go to boeason.com/actionsteps. You'll also discover other stories to help inspire you.	Tips on writing your story Example stories (from students)